Teaching Pupils with Visual Impairment

Also available

Including Children with Visual Impairment in Mainstream Schools
Mark Fox
978–1–85346–914–5

Learning Through Touch
Supporting Children with Visual Impairment and Additional Difficulties
Mike McLinden and Stephen McCall
978–1–85346–841–4

The SEN Handbook for Trainee Teachers, NQTs and Teaching Assistants
Wendy Spooner
978–1–84312–404–7

Teaching Pupils with Visual Impairment

A guide to making the school curriculum accessible

Edited by Ruth Salisbury

Routledge
Taylor & Francis Group

LONDON AND NEW YORK

First published 2008 by Routledge
2 Park Square, Milton Park, Abingdon, Oxon, OX14 4RN

Simultaneously published in the USA and Canada
by Routledge
270 Madison Ave, New York, NY 10016

Routledge is an imprint of the Taylor & Francis Group, an informa business

© 2008 Gwasg Pia Cyf

Transferred to Digital Printing 2009

Note: The right of Pia to be identified as the author of this work has been asserted by them in accordance with the Copyright, Designs and Patents Act 1988.

Typeset in Bliss by RefineCatch Limited, Bungay, Suffolk
Printed and bound in Great Britain by Bell & Bain Ltd, Glasgow

British Library Cataloguing in Publication Data
A catalogue record for this book is available from the British Library

Library of Congress Cataloging in Publication Data
A catalog record for this book has been requested

ISBN 10: 1–84312–395–9 (pbk)
ISBN 13: 978–1–84312–395–8 (pbk)

Contents

Contributors

The following people made major contributions to this book; they are listed alphabetically by surname.

Jenni Armstrong, QTVI

Jenni has worked with pupils with visual impairment for 30 years, across all age ranges and many ability levels. Her main focus has been teaching the primary curriculum, and in recent years, secondary geography. She has modified the Key Stage 2 science national curriculum test papers in England for 10 years, and has also advised for various product developments. She has published in professional journals. She is passionate that children with visual impairment should have as many real-life experiences as possible. Jenni works at St Vincent's School for the Blind in Liverpool, and thanks her colleagues for their suggestions.

Peter Bailey, BA

Peter has been the Helpline Manager since 2003 at the Modified Test Agency that produces modified versions of the national curriculum tests. During this time, he has advised over 5000 teachers, many of whom are specialist teachers for visual impairment.

Angela Beach, QTVI, Cert Ed

Angela is a specialist teacher of physical education who, for nearly 20 years, has been Physical Education Coordinator at St Vincent's School for Blind and Partially Sighted Children in Liverpool. Angela is currently Chair of the RNIB/VIEW PE Curriculum Group and a course presenter for Birmingham University on their Distance Learning visually impaired (VI) teacher's qualification.

Norman Brown, QTVI, BSc, PGCE

Norman has taught science to pupils with visual impairment for many years. He was Head of Science and Outreach Coordinator at RNIB New College. Norman has contributed to a number of publications including the *Journal of Biological Education* and publications produced by RNIB. He has recently retired from teaching but continues to modify examination papers for pupils and students with visual impairment. He also marks braille test and examination papers.

Peter Bryenton

Peter supports users of assistive technology in a specialist college for the blind and partially sighted.

Chris Edmondson, MSc, Cert Ed

Chris is a researcher and freelance management adviser. Chris previously worked as a manager in both the voluntary and public sectors and is a former school governor.

Jill Fryer, BA (Hons) LD, Ad Cert PMLD

Jill is Data Manager at Pia, with 15 years' experience in the disability field. Previously Jill worked as an FE lecturer teaching adults with severe to profound learning disabilities. Jill also worked as a braille translator and has been an active member of the Moon Forum since September 2001.

Jackie Locke, BA (Hons), PGCE, BPhil Ed. (Visual Impairment)

Jackie has taught pupils across all ages both within mainstream and special schools and has advised local authorities on the integration of pupils with visual impairment within their schools. She is currently Head of Religious Education at St Vincent's School for Blind and Partially Sighted Children in Liverpool. Jackie is also a consultant on the education of children with visual impairment for a local authority within the same area.

Hester Macdonald, BA (English), PGCE, QTVI Med (Visual Impairment and Autistic Spectrum Disorders)

Hester qualified as a teacher of English in 1994, and worked for three years in a mainstream comprehensive before moving to a specialist school for young people with visual impairment. She qualified as a teacher of the visually impaired in 1998, and continues to teach English to 'A' Level in a specialist school environment.

Linda McKinley, MA (Cantab), Dip Sp Ed (VI)

Linda has taught mathematics to students with visual impairment for many years and at RNIB New College, Worcester for 11 years. She is now a consultant in the teaching of mathematics to children and young people with visual impairment and is currently Chair of the RNIB/VIEW Mathematics Curriculum Group. She is involved with the modification of examination and test papers at Key Stage 2, GCSE and 'A' Level.

Audrey Mathias

Audrey qualified in braille in November 1997, and has supported pupils with visual impairment within mainstream schools for a local authority support service, modifying materials into braille, large print and tactile diagrams. Audrey is currently working with Pia as a braille originator and producer.

Ian Paget, BA, MEd, Dip Sp Ed (VH)

Ian recently retired from RNIB New College, Worcester where he was coordinator of ICT for many years. He continues to modify examination papers for students with visual impairment. Ian is currently chief examiner for 'A' Level ICT with the OCR Examination Board.

Valerie Price, QTVI, MIL, RSA Diploma TEFL

Val has taught Spanish and French for many years in a mainstream school that has a number of pupils with visual impairment. She is moderator for all examination boards in Spanish, Italian and Portuguese, has contributed to various publications and delivers INSET on the teaching of languages to pupils with visual impairment through her work as Secretary of RNIB/VIEW Modern Languages Curriculum Group. She works for the Inclusion Service for Visual Impairment and is Coordinator for resourced provision for learners with visual impairment at Trinity C of E High School, Manchester. Val has contributed to the book on behalf of the RNIB/VIEW Modern Languages Curriculum Group.

Ruth Salisbury, BSc

Ruth was Project Manager for modified statutory tests in Wales and England and also led the Education Team at Pia until 2006. Ruth is currently an education policy and research officer with a local authority. Ruth has developed mathematics assessment materials at the National Foundation for Educational Research (NFER) and science assessment materials for Cambridge Assessment. Ruth has an honours degree in Pschology and qualifications in British Sign Language. Ruth also has experience of working with children with moderate to profound learning difficulties in special school settings.

Maggie Simpson, Dip Art (Tapestry Weaving), Dip Ed (Art & Design)

Maggie is a teacher of art at the Royal Blind School, Edinburgh. Maggie teaches art to primary and secondary pupils up to the age of 18, and also to children with multiple disabilities and visual impairment (MDVI) at Canaan Lane Campus. She leads practical workshops for staff and parents to support pupils with visual impairment in mainstream schools.

Barbara Smith, Cert Ed, ACE (VI)

Barbara has worked in the field of visual impairment since 1992, in both mainstream and specialist settings. The majority of this experience has been in the post-16 sector, but since joining the Kent Specialist Teaching Service in a peripatetic role in 2004, her brief has extended across all ages and a wide range of settings and abilities.

Jil Timothy, MA, QTVI

Jil works as an advisory teacher for the visually impaired in Sir Ddinbych/Denbighshire. Jil enjoys writing articles for magazines and other publications and has a special interest in bilingualism and braille.

Joyce Vousden, Cert Ed, BA, QTVI

Joyce has been an advisory teacher with the Hearing and Vision Support Services in Dorset since 1994.

Sharon Williams, BEd Primary

Sharon has been involved in the project to modify the national curriculum tests in England and Wales since 1999. During this time she has contributed to maintaining the standards and principles of the provision of modified materials for pupils with visual impairment. Sharon is currently the managing director of Pia.

Sally-Anne Zimmermann, QTVI, MA (Music Education)

Sally-Anne is the Music Adviser for the Royal National Institute of the Blind. Before joining RNIB in 1994, she was a class music teacher in secondary and special schools in London, and also a violin and piano teacher. Her research interests include all aspects of assessment in the arts and are currently focused on musical development amongst pupils with profound and multiple learning difficulties.

Gwasg Pia Cyf (www.pia.co.uk)

This project is coordinated by Pia, an accessible media company specialising in accessible materials in braille, large print, Moon and audio for government departments, private companies, charities, trades unions, banks, public utility companies, universities and examination boards. Pia has modified and produced accessible versions of national curriculum tests and provided a helpline service to schools and local authorities in England and Wales since 1997. Pia is a member of the Braille Authority of the UK (BAUK), the UK Association of Braille Producers (UKABP) and the Confederation of Transcribed Information Services (COTIS).

Foreword

Some years ago, on a train, a brief discussion took place bemoaning the impending loss of modified national curriculum tests in Wales and, therefore, a standard for teachers to rely on and use as a model for modifying learning materials for pupils with visual impairment. This discussion planted a seed, which gradually grew into an idea of collecting advice, best practice and resources from experienced specialist teachers to put into a brief, accessible guide to teaching pupils with visual impairment.

Pia and colleagues in the Modified Test Agency have produced the modified versions of the national curriculum tests for many years. They have improved with time, evaluation and experience, and offered schools an example of good practice as well as valuable resources for general use in the classroom. We felt that this loss would be keenly felt in schools and were generally dispirited that our experience and knowledge would fade and become unavailable to schools. But it wasn't too late to save the information for future use.

We already had an editor, Ruth Salisbury, who has been involved with test development and modified tests for a number of years. To collate and gather the information for the book, we appointed a researcher. Chris Edmondson moved the project on at an incredible pace, recruiting specialist teachers with many years' experience teaching pupils with visual impairment in specialist and mainstream settings from across the UK to contribute their expertise. These contributors produced excellent topics and ideas, fitting writing into very busy schedules, largely during a very busy Christmas term.

The final piece in the jigsaw was RNIB. Throughout this project, which has involved writing, editing, re-writing and re-editing several times over, RNIB has given us its support. Many thanks go to our colleagues at RNIB, particularly Suzy McDonald, for giving us the confidence to forge ahead with this project.

We would also like to thank our colleagues Vivien Kilburn and Mike Joseph for their support and hard work securing the support of David Fulton Publishers for the project.

Our colleagues at Pia have provided a source of expertise, inspiration, good humour and constructive criticism throughout the life of the project. We thank them, and look forward to many more successful collaborative projects.

Sharon Williams, Managing Director, Pia.

Acknowledgements

Pia would like to thank the following for their kind permission to use material in this book:

- The Centre for Studies in Inclusive Education (CSIE) for their definition and 10 reasons for inclusion in Chapter 1
- Rebecca Harris for the reproduction of her artwork 'Positive and negative me' in Chapter 6
- The Royal National Institute of the Blind (RNIB) for permission to use images of their products in Chapters 4 and 12.

General issues

Introduction

1.1 Who will use this book?

Teaching Pupils with Visual Impairment is a guide for anyone who plays a role in the education of a child with visual impairment. It is written primarily for classroom teachers and support staff in mainstream schools, especially those who may be facing a new school year in which their class will include a pupil with visual impairment for the first time. Special Educational Needs Coordinators (SENCOs), Learning Support Coordinators (LSCs), and Inclusion Coordinators can use the information for planning and to support their colleagues. Specialist teachers for visual impairment may wish to use some of the suggestions and resources to help them support mainstream schools. This book may also offer useful information to parents of children with visual impairment who are taking an active role in the education of their child. Finally, pupils with visual impairment may find the book and accompanying CD a useful resource for playing an active role in their own education.

What is the purpose of this book?

The majority of pupils with visual impairment receive their education in mainstream schools. The experiences of pupils with visual impairment who have completed their education demonstrate that with appropriate support visual impairment is not a barrier to successful educational outcomes.

The main purpose of this book is to be a 'pick-up-and-go' guide with suggestions for making the learning environment, teaching sessions and the curriculum as accessible as possible to pupils with visual impairment. The brief for our team of writers, subject specialists with many years' experience of teaching pupils with visual impairment in both specialist and mainstream settings, was to write down the most important things they would like to tell teachers and support staff in mainstream schools about including pupils with visual impairment in each subject area.

The first part of this book presents general information on providing an appropriate learning environment for pupils with visual impairment and provides guidance on managing support and providing appropriate learning materials and equipment for pupils with visual impairment.

The second part of this book contains suggestions for making specific topics within subject areas accessible to pupils with visual impairment, many of which can be easily adapted for teaching other topics and subjects.

The final part of this book contains a directory of equipment and resources and a glossary of terms relating to visual impairment.

The accompanying CD contains a range of accessible grid papers, writing paper, music staves and map outlines in addition to a range of examples of modified learning materials. The entire text of this book is also contained as a PDF file on the CD to enable access for teachers, support staff and parents with visual impairment, and for pupils with visual impairment to access themselves.

This book does not claim to provide solutions to all the challenges faced in the classroom when working with pupils with visual impairment, and is not a substitute for advice from a specialist teacher for visual impairment. However, we hope that the suggestions and resources provided will give readers a starting point for sharing ideas and good practice.

1.2 Why is this book needed?

There are many useful books available on the subject of educating pupils with visual impairment, but they are usually theoretical, written for close study and not intended for immediate use in the classroom. We hope that this book will become dog-eared and tatty with use, and that it will be an essential part of staff libraries and a resource to turn to for ideas and inspiration. We have tried to keep advice as brief and as practical as possible and we have kept accessibility and inclusivity as our two guiding principles throughout the book.

Why inclusive education?

The Centre for Studies in Inclusive Education (CSIE) provides a definition of inclusive education in *Index for Inclusion* (Booth and Ainscow 2002):

> Inclusive education means disabled and non-disabled children and young people learning together in ordinary pre-school provision, schools, colleges and universities, with appropriate networks of support.

> Inclusion means enabling pupils to participate in the life and work of mainstream institutions to the best of their abilities, whatever their needs.

For inclusion to be effective, local authorities and schools have to adapt their approach to the curriculum, teaching support, funding mechanisms and the physical environment.

We believe that most mainstream and specialist teachers share our commitment to inclusive education. The CSIE website gives 10 reasons for inclusion:

Human rights

1. All children have the right to learn together.
2. Children should not be devalued or discriminated against by being excluded or sent away because of their disability or learning difficulty.
3. Disabled adults, describing themselves as special school survivors, are demanding an end to segregation.
4. There are no legitimate reasons to separate children for their education. Children belong together – with advantages and benefits for everyone. They do not need to be protected from each other.

Good education

5. Research shows children do better, academically and socially, in inclusive settings.
6. There is no teaching or care in a segregated school which cannot take place in an ordinary school.
7. Given commitment and support, inclusive education is a more efficient use of educational resources.

Social sense

8. Segregation teaches children to be fearful, ignorant and breeds prejudice.
9. All children need an education that will help them develop relationships and prepare them for life in the mainstream.
10. Inclusion has the potential to reduce fear and to build friendship, respect and understanding.

1.3 Visual impairment

Visual impairment has many different medical causes, and pupils' needs vary considerably. It is most important for teachers and support staff to understand the functional implications of a pupil's visual impairment, as this will affect the approaches used to meet the pupil's needs.

Partial sight

The term 'partially sighted' is used very broadly to describe pupils with visual impairment who work primarily through print. A wide range of pupils fall into this category, from those with relatively minor visual impairment through to those who may be on the margin between print and braille and whose visual condition is likely to deteriorate further. The functional implications of partial sight can be categorised into several broad headings, of which one or many may apply to different pupils.

Poor acuity
Visual acuity is the clarity or sharpness of the overall image. Both distance and near vision may be affected, but not necessarily to the same degree. Some pupils may be able to see close print but not be able to see the whiteboard, whilst others may find it easier to see objects from a distance than close up.

Central vision loss
Central vision loss affects the ability to detect fine detail. Pupils with central vision loss are likely to find tasks involving reading, writing and close observation difficult.

Peripheral vision loss
Peripheral vision loss can create the opposite effect to central vision loss, resulting in a circular tunnel-like field of vision. Pupils are likely to experience difficulties moving around and locating objects. Pupils may be able to read and write effectively, but may find scanning tasks difficult. Pupils with peripheral vision loss may be able to read small print sizes, but may need learning resource materials modified to reduce the amount of fine visual detail.

Interrupted vision
Pupils may experience irregular patches of poor vision and may pick up visual information in disjointed fragments. Severe interrupted vision can result in pupils finding many visual tasks extremely difficult, or even impossible.

Low-contrast sensitivity
Some visual conditions result in difficulties differentiating an object from its background. For these pupils, clarity and contrast may be more important than size. Lighting and colour schemes are likely to be especially significant.

Adaptability to light
Many visual conditions result in pupils experiencing difficulties adapting to variations in light. Some pupils may find bright light painful (photophobia), or may find it difficult to adjust to a change in lighting conditions.

Impaired ocular mobility
Some visual difficulties are a result of difficulties controlling the muscle functions in the eye. For example, nystagmus involves a continuous involuntary movement of the eyes, usually from side to side, which creates difficulties in focusing. Some pupils may find it hard to focus both eyes on the same object at the same time, while others may find it difficult to shift their focus between different objects and distances.

Colour loss
Many visual impairments are accompanied and compounded by colour loss. Pupils who experience colour loss may not always be aware of this, and may find it difficult to distinguish details in pictures, maps and diagrams.

Blindness

The term 'educationally blind' is often used for pupils who have insufficient sight to access print and rely on their other senses to access information. For most pupils, this involves accessing information in braille. However, do not presume that a pupil who works through braille has no useful vision at all; most braille users retain some vision, which may be useful in many aspects of everyday life.

It is important to distinguish between pupils who have had some sight in the past and those who have been blind from birth. Pupils' abilities to grasp concepts will be greatly influenced by their visual memory.

Conclusion

Visual impairment encompasses a wide range of functional implications and every pupil's needs are different. The suggestions in this book for teaching pupils with visual impairment are made by specialist teachers with experience of working with a range of pupils. However, in any given situation, no 'one size fits all' solution is available and teachers, support staff, specialist teachers, SENCOs, parents and pupils all need to work together to achieve truly inclusive education for pupils with visual impairment.

Resources

Here are some suggestions for further reading on visual conditions and associated functional implications.

- Download free fact sheets on different types of visual impairment from RNIB's website (www.rnib.org.uk/eyeinfo).
- *Spotlight on SEN: Visual Impairment* (Mason 2001).
- *Children with Visual Impairment in Mainstream Settings* (Arter *et al.* 1999).
- *Visual Impairment: Access to Education for Children and Young People* (Mason *et al.* 1997).

CHAPTER 2

The learning environment

2.1 Physical environment

An accessible physical environment does much to reduce barriers to learning for pupils with visual impairment. It is vital to involve pupils in as much as possible of the planning, preparation and adaptation of the school environment. Parents, the SENCO and the sensory support service are all good sources of help and should be involved on an ongoing basis.

In the school

- Familiarise pupils with the school site before starting at the school. Pupils with visual impairment may need more visits than other pupils.

- Arrange a risk assessment of the school site in relation to individual pupils' needs; involve the local authority health and safety officer, the SENCO, the pupil and the pupil's parents.

- Signs should be clear, well placed and easily visible – consider tactile, braille or large print signs as appropriate.

- Steps, edges and changes in level may need to be highlighted with yellow or white paint lines.

- Handrails assist with mobility.

- Tactile trails using textured materials or 'bumps' applied to walls at hand height can be easily followed for routes to toilets, dining halls, etc.

- Different floor coverings for different areas of the school and classroom and on stairways help indicate a change of environment.

- Prevent accidents by keeping stairs, corridors and doorways free from obstruction.

- Clear panels on doors (especially swing doors) help ensure people can be seen approaching from the other side of the door and can help avoid collisions.

- Playgrounds can be made accessible with 'quiet' and 'active' areas, shaded areas for pupils with photophobia (light sensitivity) and scented and tactile plants to provide sensory experiences. Ensure any playground games such as hopscotch grids are clearly painted and maintained.

- Position displays at an accessible level (see also 4.8 Visual displays).

- Position coat pegs and lockers so that they are easy for pupils to locate, close to the door is helpful.

In the classroom

- Lighting levels may need to be high for some pupils, while some pupils may be photophobic and need lower lighting levels. Check this with all pupils, parents and the SENCO.
- Task lighting (i.e. lighting positioned to fall directly onto a pupil's area of work, perhaps from a spot or desk lamp) may be required, as will good ambient lighting.
- Window blinds help reduce glare.
- Consider removing or covering reflective surfaces to reduce glare.
- Avoid standing in front of windows when teaching as pupils may see no more than a silhouette; this is good practice in general.
- Position pupils with a visual impairment in the most suitable position for maximum access to whiteboards, OHP screens, flipcharts, etc. (but NOT apart from other pupils).
- Use a clear contrast when writing for the class, e.g. a black pen on a whiteboard; avoid using colour and pens with insufficient ink.
- Provide individual copies of anything presented on a whiteboard or overhead projector.
- All pupils should have individual copies of textbooks or worksheets; avoid sharing copies between pupils.
- Avoid worksheets and books with writing positioned over coloured backgrounds.
- Reading stands or desk boards are useful to attain a good reading or working position, but should not limit interaction with other pupils.
- Additional space may be needed for equipment, large print papers, etc.
- Ensure additional equipment does not cause a hazard with trailing cables or by blocking walkways.
- Prevent accidents by avoiding storing books, boxes or other items that could form obstacles on the floor of the classroom.
- Provide real objects for illustrating lessons; these are useful for pupils with visual impairment to hold and touch and can make lessons more interesting for the whole class.
- Consistency is crucial; always keep things in the same place and avoid changing the layout of the classroom.

Resources

- Bumpons, simple raised bumps supplied on self-adhesive sheets in a range of sizes and colours for marking different equipment, are available from RNIB (www.rnib.org.uk) and Disability Supplies (www.disabilitysupplies.co.uk).
- Tactile signs are available from a range of suppliers (see 18.1 Directory of suppliers).
- Reading stands and desk boards are available from a range of stationery suppliers.

- RNIB's 'Exploring access in mainstream' (Naish *et al.* 2004) is a folder of information for staff in mainstream schools; it deals with access and adaptations to the physical environment for children with visual impairment.

2.2 Social environment

Simple and thoughtful action can do much to ensure that pupils with visual impairment can fully access the social life of the school community. This is as important for pupils' development as access to academic activity.

- Ensure that all staff, including lunchtime supervisors and school governors, are aware of pupils' individual needs.

- Address pupils by name before asking a question or giving an instruction.

- Arrange awareness and information sessions to ensure that other pupils and staff are well informed about visual impairment, e.g. visits to the school from organisations such as Guide Dogs for the Blind Association.

- Read out material presented on a whiteboard.

- Within the class, position pupils with visual impairment to allow full interaction with other pupils.

- Provide opportunities for sighted pupils to learn skills and games usually offered only to pupils with visual impairment, such as learning braille and playing goalball (see 15.4 Team games).

- Encourage and enable pupils with visual impairment to participate in school trips, PE, playground games, after school activities, plays and assemblies.

- Encourage and enable pupils with visual impairment to enjoy meals and breaks with their peers, not in a separate area with support staff or with younger pupils.

- Be aware of the dangers of overincluding pupils and applying too much pressure, e.g. by asking for answers to too many questions, etc.

- Be aware of the dangers of being overprotective; encourage pupils to develop independence.

Resources

- Local authority sensory support services offer support with pupils' social development and offer awareness and information training for school staff and pupils.

- To arrange a visit from Guide Dogs for the Blind Association, contact your local branch; contact details are available at www.guidedogs.co.uk

2.3 Trips and visits

Pupils with visual impairment should always be included in trips and visits. For maximum benefit and impact, some specific preparation is necessary.

Planning

It is advisable to visit a location before taking any group there. When the group includes pupils with visual impairment this is especially important, as there are additional issues to be considered.

Some locations will already be prepared for visitors with a variety of access requirements, so it is worth finding out what is actually available. They may have large print and/or braille guides, braille labels or signs, audio guides and special facilities for handling artefacts and artworks. Know pupils' needs and ask if and how these needs can be met.

A risk assessment is vital when taking pupils with any access requirement on a trip. A specialist teacher for visual impairment will be able to advise on what to look for.

Consider the accessibility of the venue. Will pupils with visual impairment be able to move around independently or will they require sighted guide assistance? Is there a member of support staff available who has the necessary skills to guide pupils with visual impairment in an unfamiliar environment? How will this level of supervision affect the dynamics of the group?

When considering the aims of the visit it is important to think of the various ways these aims can be met. Instead of the natural tendency to concentrate on what will be seen, think about the experience in a multi-sensory way; what will be heard, smelt, felt, for instance?

The trip

Transport is likely to affect the level of support required. Pupils with visual impairment may need more support if using public transport.

Weather conditions may affect the level of vision. On dull days, some pupils with visual impairment may find it much harder to see clearly, whilst for others, bright days with the sun low in the sky and a lot of glare will reduce their vision considerably and may even cause them pain. Remind parents to provide dark glasses or hats in the summer.

Some venues may, of necessity, be dimly lit and again this may create added difficulty for some pupils. It is important to be aware of the effects of different lighting levels when planning support. Ensuring that support assistants are equipped with a torch to provide additional local light may be a useful idea.

Pupils need to be appropriately equipped to complete tasks during the visit. Whereas the rest of the group may have printed worksheets and pencils, pupils with visual impairment may need a different format for reading information and a different method for recording responses.

Conclusion

With careful planning and appropriate support, pupils with visual impairment can be fully included in trips and visits.

Resources

Museums, Galleries and Heritage Sites: Improving Access for Blind and Partially Sighted People, The Talking Images Guide (RNIB and Vocaleyes 2003) gives a practical overview of all areas of access for visitors with visual impairment (available to download at www.rnib.org.uk).

2.4 Mobility, orientation and life skills

Pupils with severe visual impairment receive mobility training from a specialist mobility officer. This is a legal requirement and continues throughout pupils' education, but many everyday classroom activities can help to build and develop the skills and confidence pupils will need. Here are some simple ways to encourage increasing independence and mobility for pupils with visual impairment.

- Establish close collaboration with the mobility specialist in the local authority.
- Encourage body awareness with finger play games, rhymes about body parts, partner games making each other into shapes, walking around each other with shoulders touching, etc.
- Divide routes around the school into small segments and help pupils to learn one part of the route at a time, rather than trying to learn it all at once.
- Use 'hand clues' such as plastic shapes glued to the back of pupils' chairs, fronts of storage drawers and by coat pegs for easy identification; use tactile symbols or different textured panels on doors.
- Help pupils to practise sound location skills by playing games; find 'noisy toys' such as musical boxes and place them in different locations, varying height as well as direction, and encourage pupils to find the toys by sound.
- Encourage pupils to move around the school independently once familiar with the site; they may need assistance or may need to be allowed to leave class a few minutes early to avoid crowded corridors and stairs.
- Allow time before or after school for pupils to use a walking machine or similar aid.
- Encourage pupils to put away their own materials and equipment, and to take a full part in tidying up the classroom with other pupils.
- Make pupils 'room monitors', e.g. in charge of the lights.
- Ask pupils to take their turn fetching or returning the register, materials or equipment from the resources room or other areas of the school.
- Ask pupils to take messages to other staff in different parts of the building.

Resources

- The Sensory Company (www.thesensorycompany.co.uk) supplies a range of multi-sensory products including equipment for sensory rooms and sensory gardens.
- TFH Special Needs Toys (www.specialneedstoys.co.uk) supplies a range of multi-sensory toys and texture panels.

2.5 Transition at 11+

The move from primary to secondary school is one of the biggest changes to happen during a pupil's education. Visual impairment can make this transition even more difficult and traumatic without careful planning. Making the transition from primary to secondary generally involves moving from a small to a large site, learning a set of new and more complicated routes and familiarisation with several classrooms rather than one main classroom in primary school.

The school environment

An environmental audit establishes a building's accessibility for people with visual impairment. Many local associations for the blind undertake this, or RNIB can also offer this service. An environmental audit highlights such issues as lighting levels, glare, contrast, changes in levels, surfaces underfoot and general layout. A detailed report suggests ways in which the environment can be improved.

Simple and inexpensive features include highlighting the edges of all steps and stairs, ensuring that the diffusers on strip lights are kept clean, ensuring that blinds are all in working order and providing clear signage at eye level. Recommendations are also made for improvements such as contrasting colours for doors or door frames and door furniture.

Preparation

Many schools now organise taster days for pupils about to join secondary school. It is important for pupils with visual impairment to join with their friends who may be going to the same school on these occasions, and also to meet new peers joining from the wider area. It is also a good idea to arrange at least one additional visit on their own or in a small group for orientation purposes.

SENCOs and specialist teachers

Good communication between SENCOs will ensure that all relevant information is passed on. The specialist teacher for visual impairment should also be working towards this goal.

Parents

Parents are likely to want to know that the needs of their child can be met and may, understandably, be persistent in their enquiries. Effective communication, e.g. a meeting between SENCOs, parents and the specialist teacher, can help address parents' concerns.

In-service training (INSET)

Specialist teachers are likely to be able to offer staff INSET to prepare for the challenges of including pupils with visual impairment. This can help to allay fears and suggest positive strategies for classroom management. It is vital that support staff, who will work closely with pupils, have the opportunity to learn about visual conditions, their implications and appropriate methods of working.

Equipment

Equipment used at primary school may no longer be suitable in the new environment. For example, a large video magnifier may have worked well in the primary school classroom, but would be impractical when every lesson is in a different room. This is an area where the specialist teacher can provide valuable advice and, possibly, support an application for something more appropriate (see 4.10 Access technology).

Transport and travel

A major concern when selecting a secondary school may be the journey involved. Independent travellers would benefit from the help of a mobility officer to learn the new routes and how to navigate them safely. If taxi transport is appropriate, this should be organised with the local authority well in advance.

2.6 Transition at 16+

For all pupils, decisions made at this stage of their education can influence the rest of their lives. For pupils with visual impairment, there are many additional factors to consider.

Thinking ahead

Reviews from the age of 14 should begin the process of planning for what will happen at age 16. A full transition plan should be prepared, clearly defining the roles and responsibilities of all concerned. Pupils and parents should visit as many of the possible choices as they can, and ask probing questions about the courses on offer and the support available.

The options

There is usually a range of choices available. This may include:

- the sixth form of the current school
- the sixth form of another school
- a sixth-form college
- a college of further education
- a specialist college for students with visual impairment.

Factors to consider

To choose the most appropriate destination, a number of factors should be considered, including:

- the aims of the learner
- the available curriculum and its suitability for the learner
- the support available

- the accessibility of the school or college, both in terms of getting there and of moving around the site.

Funding

In the UK, sixth-form colleges and FE colleges are bound by the terms of the Disability Discrimination Act (1995), and must make 'reasonable adjustments' to meet the needs of students with visual impairment. However, how they do this varies considerably in different areas. Some local authorities include a post–16 service in their sensory support service, usually charging the college at an hourly rate. Some colleges rely on their own expertise. Funding mechanisms should be explored when considering colleges to ensure appropriate support is given.

Specialist provision

If a specialist college is the preferred route, local authorities will need to be convinced that the pupil's needs cannot be met in a mainstream setting. The cost of specialist provision, especially if it is residential, is high and a good case will need to be made to justify the expense. A pupil who has succeeded in mainstream school is unlikely to be funded for a specialist college unless a specific need, such as the development of independent life skills or mastery of specialist technology, is a priority.

Conclusion

Plan ahead: explore every option well in advance and ask plenty of questions before making a decision.

Resources

- For further advice on post–16 education for young people with visual impairment, including details of specialist colleges, visit RNIB's student website at www.rnib.org.uk/student
- The Association of National Specialist Colleges website (www.natspec.org.uk/expertise.php) has a 'college finder' function with contact details for specialist colleges for students with a range of special needs.

CHAPTER 3

Managing support

3.1 The specialist teacher for visual impairment

In the UK, local authorities have sensory support services, which include qualified specialist teachers for visual impairment, also known as qualified teachers for the visually impaired (QTVIs). They are there to help and to enable schools to include pupils with visual impairment in every aspect of the curriculum.

Assessments

Specialist teachers often complete an assessment of functional vision and provide the school with a report outlining the challenges to be faced and strategies for dealing with them (see 5.3 Assessment of functional vision). They do not make a medical diagnosis but usually liaise with the appropriate medical professionals.

Visits

The frequency of visits is determined by pupils' needs, and each service has its own criteria for making these decisions. Usually this is only a guide and additional visits can be requested if there are any concerns.

During a visit the specialist teacher may observe the pupil in class to assess accessibility to the curriculum and how the pupil is coping. Strategies may be suggested to assist teachers, support staff and pupils.

On occasions, the specialist teacher might meet with a pupil on a one-to-one basis. This could be for additional assessments, to discuss progress from the pupil's perspective, to discuss social and emotional issues relating to visual impairment or to carry out specific teaching agreed with the school (e.g. braille, touch typing or the use of specialist equipment).

It is useful if there is an opportunity for the class teacher or the SENCO to discuss any issues raised during the visit. Schools should usually receive a report about the visit.

Training

Specialist teachers usually offer training to staff at the school, on a whole-school basis, to a small group or even to individuals. This is particularly valuable the first time a school admits a pupil with visual impairment. It is also helpful for other pupils to have a visual awareness session to help them understand the situation.

Many sensory support services run courses for support staff working with pupils with visual impairment, or recommend other courses running in the area.

Annual reviews

Specialist teachers often attend annual reviews or provide reports to update all parties on matters relating to a pupil's functional vision. This is particularly important at any transition point where advice on appropriate placements may be needed.

Conclusion

Specialist teachers are there to support the whole school as well as pupils with visual impairment. They can provide a valuable link between the pupil, the home, the school and other relevant professionals.

3.2 The Special Educational Needs Coordinator

The Special Educational Needs Coordinator (SENCO) is the 'hub' of all things relating to special educational needs within the school. As such, the SENCO is not expected to know about every special need that is encountered but can access information from many sources. Most SENCOs have at least one area of expertise, but interact with external agencies for support in other fields.

The SENCO's role within the school

Some schools have a full-time SENCO with little or no mainstream teaching responsibility. The SENCO is likely to undertake small group work, particularly if the school has a large special educational needs (SEN) department. In other schools, the SENCO is released from classroom duties to undertake the SENCO work, and in some cases a part-time SENCO is employed. Generally speaking, the larger the school, the more time a SENCO needs to deal with the responsibilities of this role.

The SENCO and pupils

The SENCO should be aware of every pupil within the school who has any special educational need, or other additional need. The greater a pupil's need, the more involvement the SENCO generally has. The SENCO is involved in writing individual education plans (IEPs) and also completing much of the paperwork for applications for statements of special educational need, funding, etc.

The SENCO and other staff

The SENCO often manages support staff within the school, as they are aware of the individual needs of pupils who require this type of support. In many schools, the SENCO is the contact point between outside agencies and the school, and is likely to be the one who maintains records of visits from visiting professionals and communicates their recommendations to other staff. The SENCO is usually a member of the senior management team and is, as such, involved in policy decisions. It is certainly their responsibility to ensure that SEN issues receive an appropriate profile within overall plans.

Conclusion

SENCOs have a vital role to play within a school, liaising with outside agencies, worried parents, anxious teachers and harassed support staff. However, the main focus is ensuring the best possible opportunities for all pupils within their brief.

3.3 Working with support staff

Support staff (including learning support assistants, teaching assistants, teaching associates, nursery nurses, etc.) are a valuable resource for ensuring equal access for pupils with visual impairment. However, their time needs to be managed effectively if the best use is to be made of their support.

Support or help?

The role of support staff is not to do the work for the pupil. They are there to enable the pupil to access and complete the work. The success of support can be measured by how independent the pupil becomes. Effective support should reduce, or at least change, over time. Sometimes it seems the easy option to complete a task for the pupil; it may even seem unkind to expect a degree of independence. However, support should encourage pupils to assume responsibility for learning and decision-making.

Knowing pupils' needs

It is vital that support staff have full information about the pupils they are supporting. The SENCO and/or the class teacher should provide this information. Clarification and additional information may also be obtained from the specialist teacher. If specific training is available in the area, enable and encourage support staff to attend even if it is costly, as it will give them a greater understanding of visual impairment, which they will be able to apply in the classroom. Support staff should encourage pupils to express their own needs, to be able to ask when something is inaccessible and to explain why.

Working alongside pupils

Support staff working alongside pupils should know which side is the best position, e.g. if the pupil has better vision in one eye than the other, that is the side from which to work. Support staff need to know what is required in a particular lesson. Are they there to scribe from the board, to assist with the navigation of resources, to read out text that is too small or to act as a practical assistant? The teacher should explain the purpose of an activity and discuss with the support staff how pupils with visual impairment can be helped to achieve this.

It is essential that changes to planned lessons are discussed beforehand rather than announced at the last minute, otherwise support staff will have to quickly decide how best to make the lesson accessible. There are usually more ways than one of reaching the same goal; the route used by the rest of the class may not be appropriate for someone with reduced or no vision. The specialist teacher will be able to advise on this.

If support staff are to act as amanuenses, taking down information from the board, it may be helpful to equip them with a small whiteboard. This is reusable and can serve to provide information almost simultaneously with that going onto the board for the rest of the class.

Acting as a practical assistant

There are some activities that may be very difficult for pupils with visual impairment to perform safely. These are likely to be in the sciences and technologies. Using machinery, heating over a naked flame and dealing with very hot liquids are examples. Advice appropriate to the needs of a particular pupil may be obtained from a specialist teacher. There are often ways in which apparently impossible barriers can be overcome.

Pupils should be fully involved in the process and should have the opportunity to explore any equipment safely and to have the equipment explained. As far as possible, support staff should follow the instructions of the pupil, but this can only happen if time has been taken beforehand to provide that understanding. Support staff may need, for example, to light the Bunsen burner when directed by the pupil, but it should be the pupil who turns on the gas if possible.

Fine measurement and marking may also be challenging for pupils with visual impairment. Often the task can be modified to require a more appropriate degree of accuracy, or enhanced markings provided. If this is not possible, pupils should develop the ability to explain exactly what support is required. Guidelines published by examination boards provide explanations of the type and degree of practical support that can be provided in a variety of situations.

Adapting resources

Support staff are often required to adapt learning resource materials. If pupils are to access appropriately modified learning materials at the same time as the rest of the class, forward planning is vital. For the majority of pupils with visual impairment, simple photocopy enlarging is not the most appropriate solution. If materials need to be modified for individual pupils, this will take time. This is particularly the case when tactile resources are required. For support staff to modify work, it is important for all parties to understand what is wanted and by when.

It is often helpful to have one member of support staff with overall responsibility for the management of resources for all pupils with visual impairment. It is important that time is identified and included in timetables for this important aspect of their work. If resources are accessible, pupils will be more able to work independently thus reducing the need for support in the classroom. See Chapter 4 Materials and equipment for more information on adapting resources.

The teacher/support relationship

Remember that support staff cannot assume the role of a teacher. Support staff are not there to teach, but to ensure that pupils are able to access the lesson. If there are questions regarding the content of the lesson, or any lack of understanding, pupils should ask the teacher. It is also important that support staff are not regarded as a natural 'partner' for pupils when the class is working in pairs. When placing pupils in groups, support staff should not be included, as it is important for pupils to learn how to work together.

Support staff working closely with individual pupils are likely to get to know that pupil well. Be prepared to listen to their feedback.

Review

Support is not the same as help. Help disables; support enables. Teaching and support staff should plan ahead so that time and support can be used effectively.

Resources

Individual whiteboards are available from stationery suppliers. Alternatively, make a whiteboard by laminating a sheet of paper and use a dry marker that can be wiped clean.

3.4 Individual education plans

An individual education plan (IEP) builds on the curriculum that a pupil with additional needs is following. The IEP is designed to list and describe the strategies being used to meet each pupil's needs.

Pupils with visual impairment should have an IEP to ensure that they have access to all areas of the curriculum and that their specific areas of need are properly assessed, met and monitored. One IEP covers all needs to enable access to the curriculum and school life: educational, mobility, support, special aids or equipment, etc.

IEPs include short-term achievable targets to help pupils plan for and achieve success. The targets are set with the involvement and agreement of pupils and should not be too numerous – three to four at one time. The teaching strategies to be used in supporting pupils in meeting the targets are also included.

IEPs should be reviewed at least twice in every academic year, although in the case of specific need such as visual impairment, reviews can usefully be more frequent. The reviews should involve pupils wherever possible and ideally include parents. Ensure that school managers are aware of the needs identified in the IEP.

If a pupil has to be withdrawn from lessons, e.g. for mobility and/or independence training, plan this for a different time each week to ensure that one subject is not regularly missed.

Review

A good IEP will include outcomes and also the date for the next review. It will also be in regular use and accessible to teachers, support staff, pupils and parents.

Resources

The DfES website for teachers (www.teachernet.gov.uk) includes further information on IEPs.

CHAPTER 4

Materials and equipment

4.1 Preparing learning resource materials

Many teachers are faced with the challenge of preparing and presenting learning resource materials to one or two pupils with visual impairment within a class of sighted pupils. There are a number of general strategies that can minimise the amount of work for teachers, support staff and pupils.

- Seek advice from a specialist teacher to provide the most appropriate materials for each pupil; this information should also be available in IEPs.

- Forward planning is essential to ensure support staff have adequate time to modify materials.

- For support staff to modify learning materials, it is important for all parties to understand what is wanted and by when; teachers and support staff should work together to identify the objectives of the learning materials, and time should be included in support staff timetables for modification work.

- Consider producing learning materials for ALL pupils in an accessible font size and type (minimum 14 point); this will also benefit pupils with learning difficulties such as dyslexia, and pupils whose visual impairment is not yet diagnosed.

- Use a word processor to prepare learning materials where possible; separate copies can then be prepared and saved for individual pupils.

- Provide electronic copies of learning materials to enable pupils to complete work using a word processor; this also allows teachers to add comments later in the appropriate place in the work, in a format appropriate to each pupil.

- Electronic learning materials can be sent to pupils by email, with the advantage that parents, teachers and support staff are able to read the communications even if the work is sent to a braille user. Sending learning materials in advance of a lesson will enable pupils and support staff to prepare for the lesson.

- Pupils with visual impairment often require additional time to process information and complete tasks. Consider modifying the task, e.g. pupils with visual impairment may demonstrate understanding of a mathematical concept by solving fewer problems.

- Remember that accessible learning materials enable pupils to work independently, thus reducing the need for support in the classroom.

Resources

Before spending time adapting published learning resource materials, it is worth finding out if someone else has already produced a modified version, even if the format is not the same as you require. Here are some suggestions for finding materials in modified formats.

- Revealweb (www.revealweb.org.uk) is a database of resources in modified formats, as well as an increasing number of electronic and digital versions.

- Braille versions of children's books are available from ClearVision (www.clearvisionproject.org). ClearVision books all have braille, print and pictures making them suitable for sharing. ClearVision also has tactile books available to loan.

- National Blind Children's Society (www.nbcs.org.uk) produces braille books on request at the cost of the original.

- The BECTA VI Forum (http://lists.becta.org.uk/mailman/listinfo/vi-forum) is a useful source of advice on issues relating to teaching pupils with visual impairment in general, and provides a forum for sharing accessible copies of learning resource materials.

4.2 Accessible print

Many pupils with visual impairment can access printed materials. However, to ensure accessibility a range of adaptations and modifications may be required, which will vary considerably depending on the nature of visual impairment and the needs of individual pupils.

Photocopy enlargement or reduction

Enlarging or reducing materials using a photocopier may be appropriate for pupils who simply require materials in a different size, with no further modification. Accessible photocopy materials require a good-quality original and a good-quality photocopier. Pupils' preferences for paper size should also be considered; some pupils dislike using large paper as it may be physically difficult to work with and some pupils dislike feeling 'different' to their peers. Some pupils may prefer A3 portrait enlargements cut down to A4 landscape.

Modified print

Visual layout and the amount of information presented are as important as print size to many pupils. Many learning materials are highly visual with illustrations, complex diagrams, a variety of font styles and sizes, colour backgrounds, etc. These features may need to be omitted or simplified for pupils with visual impairment. See 4.5 Modifying learning resource materials for more information.

Use of colour

Photocopying materials into black and white, onto coloured paper or using coloured overlays may increase accessibility for some pupils. To produce materials in different coloured print from a hard copy, they will need to be scanned into a computer and then the colour can be changed.

Checklist for accessible print

Here are some guidelines for producing accessible print materials:

- Font type – Use a clear font style such as Arial, Tahoma or Tiresias; avoid fonts that are light in appearance or use curved lines; avoid using more than one font type within a document.

- Font size – Consider producing all learning materials in size 14 point, RNIB's recommended minimum font size. For pupils who cannot access size 14 point, bespoke learning materials will need to be produced. For pupils who need to use a font size greater than 24 point, or whose visual impairment is deteriorating, alternative access methods may be required such as electronic format with speech synthesisers, video magnifiers or braille. Some pupils with visual impairment may require small print; work with a specialist teacher to establish a preferred font size.

- Formatting – Avoid using italics, underlining and upper case letters for continuous text; some pupils may require bold or semi-bold print.

- Justification – Avoid full justification with straight right margins; left justify text, as pupils who are unable to scan pages will start at the left of the page.

- Spacing – Leave space before and after paragraphs and illustrations. Remember, pupils with visual impairment often require additional space for handwriting.

- Use clear contrast – Use black text on white or cream paper unless individual pupils require alternative colours. Avoid colour print and backgrounds where possible; if colour is used, ensure as strong a contrast as possible.

- Backgrounds – Avoid materials with text superimposed over illustrations or graphics.

- Paper – Avoid paper with a gloss or shiny surface as this can cause glare; use a matt finished paper wherever possible.

- Layout – Keep page design as clear and uncluttered as possible – illustrations, drawings, tables and graphs may need to be modified or simplified (see 4.5 Modifying learning resource materials).

Resources

- For more information on accessible print, see *See It Right* (RNIB 2006), RNIB's guidance on making publications accessible to people with visual impairment.

- The Tiresias font is available to purchase from www.tiresias.org/fonts

- The accompanying CD has a large print version of this book in PDF format. The large print version is available for teachers, support staff, parents or pupils with visual impairment to access the contents of this book. It is also an example of an accessible large print text document.

4.3 Braille

Braille is a tactile writing and reading system based on a grid of six raised dots called a cell. Each dot is numbered from one to six, which helps describe the letter pattern to the learner, e.g. 'Dots 1 and 4 form the letter C'.

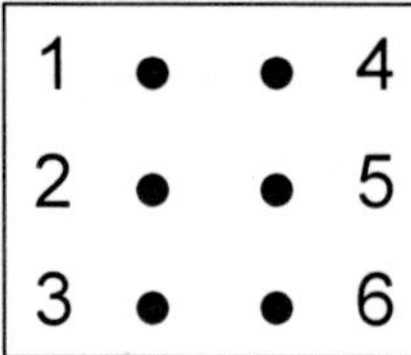

Figure 4.1   Braille cell

Grade 1 braille is the simplest form, where each braille cell represents a single print letter. Grade 1 braille also includes numbers and punctuation. Numbers are formed by placing a numeral sign in front of the letters A to J; A to I represent 1 to 9 and J represents 0. Punctuation marks have their own dot pattern, all of which have to be learnt.

Grade 2 braille uses contractions (abbreviations or short forms) of many words and letter combinations. Contractions include short forms, such as 'bl' for 'blind', as well as single cell contractions for some words such as 'and', 'for', 'the' and 'knowledge'. As a result of these contractions, grade 2 braille uses much less space than grade 1 braille. Here are some comparisons of grade 1 and grade 2 braille:

Table 4.1

Word	Grade 1	Grade 2
blind		
and		
for		
the		
knowledge		

Grade 2 braille takes much longer to learn than grade 1 braille, but once learnt many users find grade 2 braille quicker and easier to read and write. There are also versions of the braille code for mathematics, science, music, computer code and languages other than English. These codes are usually taught after learners are proficient at using the standard braille code and specialist knowledge is needed to teach these versions.

Braille is produced commercially using braille translation software that converts the text characters on screen into the braille equivalent. The document is then printed out using a braille embosser.

Braille can be produced manually with a Perkins brailler, which is a mechanical machine with nine keys similar to a simple typewriter. Many schools and pupils use Perkins braillers, which are very reliable, although noisy. Placing a rubber mat underneath the machine can reduce noise.

The paper used in Perkins braillers is 11″ braille paper, which fits exactly into the machine and is heavy enough to produce good lasting dots; A4 braille paper is also available. Ordinary paper can be used but is not encouraged as lightweight paper produces unstable dots that are easily squashed, especially with repeated readings.

Figure 4.2   Perkins brailler © RNIB

Electronic machines, such as braille notetakers are also available (see 4.10 Access technology). Braille notetakers have the advantage of being portable, but are very expensive.

Additional time will always be required for reading braille; even the most competent braille user reads more slowly than a sighted person.

Support staff and specialist teachers teach braille to individual pupils on a one-to-one basis. Thoughtful planning, preparation and advance discussion between the class teacher and the support team can do much to assist the braille learner.

The Braille Alphabet

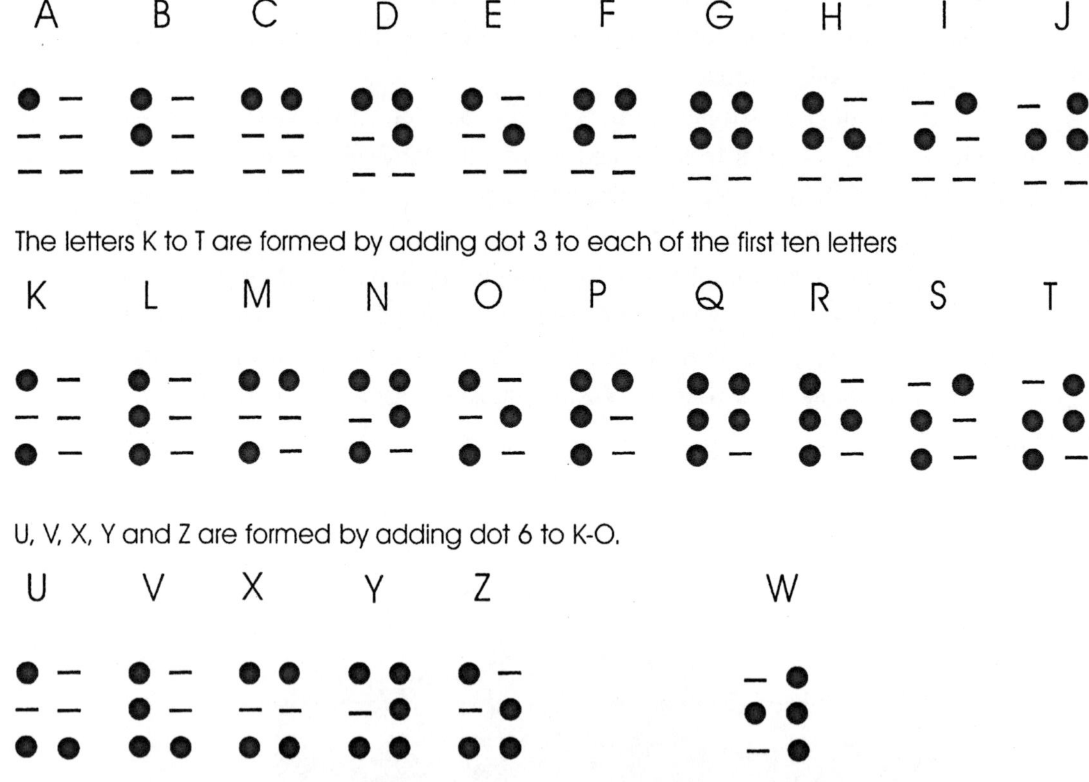

The letters K to T are formed by adding dot 3 to each of the first ten letters

U, V, X, Y and Z are formed by adding dot 6 to K-O.

Figure 4.3

Resources

- See 18.1 Directory of suppliers for Perkins machines, braille paper and other equipment.
- Download free braille fonts from www.tsbvi.edu/Education/fonts.html

4.4 Tactile diagrams

For pupils with severe visual impairment, tactile diagrams may be essential for accessing information. Pupils with visual impairment may find the concept of diagrammatic and pictorial representation of the real world difficult to grasp. However, diagrams are an essential part of pupils' learning and pupils should be given the opportunity to explore and enjoy tactile diagrams.

Tactile diagrams are useful when:

- an image is not easily described in words
- shape and pattern are vital to understanding the concept
- scale is important (maps, etc.)
- the real object is unavailable (e.g. an animal)
- pupils have little or no sight but have some tactile skill.

Tactile diagrams are not useful when:

- a shape is easily described in words
- the diagram is merely a visual embellishment and the information is already in the text
- intricate detail is essential to the image
- a real object or model is easily available
- pupils have not been taught how to interpret tactile diagrams.

Tactile books

Tactile materials are particularly useful for picture books with younger pupils, e.g. using a piece of fake fur for a dog, using aluminium foil to represent metal.

Simple line drawings

Simple line drawings can be made with spur wheels on braille paper, thermoform plastic or drawing film.

Heat swell diagrams

Heat swell diagrams are originated by printing or photocopying a black and white image onto specially coated paper and feeding it through a heat machine that raises all the black areas. Heat swell paper diagrams are outline diagrams so are ideal for simple raised diagrams such as flow charts and number lines. They are also ideal for pupils who are able to access black outlines using their residual vision.

Thermoformed diagrams

Thermoformed diagrams are produced from a tactile original made as a collage, using materials such as wire, string and sandpaper. The collage is copied onto plastic sheets in a vacuum-forming thermoform machine. The advantage of thermoformed diagrams is that different depths, as well as textures, may be created. This is useful when building pie charts and graphs or for more complex diagrams. Diagrams can also be copied onto drawing film in a thermoform machine. Pupils can make tactile marks on the drawing film using a stylus or ballpoint pen.

Embossed braille paper diagrams

Simple diagrams, such as tables and charts, can be produced on braille paper. Pictograms can be produced on braille paper using the ⠿ (for) sign. Tiger embossers produce simple diagrams using raised dots on standard braille paper, and enable text and diagrams to be embossed on the same page.

Audio tactile diagrams

A recent development in tactile diagrams is audio tactile technology. Tactile overlays are placed on a touch screen device that plugs into a standard computer. As pupils feel the diagram they can press down on different parts of the diagram to hear pre-programmed audio, such as a sound effect or spoken description. Ready-made tactile diagrams are available and specialist software enables users to produce their own diagrams.

Design tips

Work together with your local sensory support service to provide tactile diagrams for non-print users. Here are some design tips to think about when designing a tactile image.

- Reproducing visual graphics in tactile form without modification is unlikely to be effective. Tactile diagrams should be designed specifically for the tactile user, presenting key features only.
- Too much detail can make a diagram as worthless as too little; be careful to find the right balance.
- Attempt to convey the meaning of the image; a tactile diagram doesn't always need to look like the original visual image.
- If a diagram is very difficult to modify, consider using written description and/or real objects and models.
- A complex visual image, e.g. with many layers or features, may be more accessible if it is presented as a series of separate tactile diagrams with a different diagram for each layer or feature.
- Tactile diagrams should be accompanied by written description to provide context and help users locate the key features.
- Use a title to provide context and help pupils position the page the right way up.
- Letters are easier to remember than numbers when using a key.
- Braille fonts available to download from the internet can be used to convert text to grade 1 braille for labels at no cost.
- Pupils with visual impairment often have difficulties understanding scale. Include a scale marker to show the size of an object.
- 5mm separation between lines and objects is needed for tactile discrimination.
- Objects can be easier to identify when they are solid rather than just an outline.
- Very simple images, e.g. basic charts, can be produced on a braille embosser.
- Avoid smudging on swell paper by coating the finished diagram with hairspray or fixing spray available from art and craft suppliers.
- Consider adding tactile materials, e.g. feathers, fur, etc., onto tactile diagrams to add texture and interest.
- Pupils with residual vision may find black or coloured outlines useful instead of relying on tactile skills alone.
- Tactile diagrams can be coloured to make them more attractive and accessible to all pupils.
- Colour ink does not rise on swell paper diagrams, and so can be used to produce print labels without confusing the tactile user.

- It is helpful if tactile and large print diagrams are modified in the same way so that pupils using the different formats can access the same information.

- Test the images yourself with your eyes closed. If you can't feel your way around the object, it is unlikely that pupils will be able to.

- Encourage all pupils to make tactile diagrams and then test them out using blindfolds with sighted pupils. This helps all pupils understand the issues facing tactile diagram users.

- Ask pupils for their feedback on tactile diagrams. They might suggest some simple changes that will help them access diagrams.

Resources

- Ask the specialist teacher about tactile diagram training courses for support staff.

- The National Centre for Tactile Diagrams (www.nctd.org.uk) has a large catalogue of tactile diagrams available to purchase and also offers training courses. Their website has information on designing and producing tactile diagrams.

- *Thermoformed Tactile Diagrams – A Manual for Teachers and Technicians* (Hinton 1988), available free on RNIB's website, is a useful guide to designing and producing thermoform diagrams.

- Heat swell paper and Zy-Fuse heaters for raising images are available from Zychem Limited (www.zychem.co.uk).

- Thermoform machines are available from CR Clarke (www.crclarke.co.uk). Thermoform plastic and drawing film are available from CR Clarke and from RNIB.

- Tiger embossers are available from Force 10 (www.forcetenco.co.uk).

- Audio tactile devices, which comprise a touch screen device, tactile diagrams and accompanying software, include the 'T3 tactile tablet', available from Zychem Limited (www.zychem.co.uk) and the IVEO™, available from Force 10 (www.forcetenco.co.uk).

- Free braille fonts are available to download from the Texas School for the Blind and Visually Impaired website (www.tsbvi.edu/Education/fonts.html).

- Spur wheels are available from RNIB.

4.5 Modifying learning resource materials

Modifying learning resource materials for pupils using modified print or braille is a time-consuming and skilled task. Many learning resource materials have a highly visual layout with diagrams, charts, tables, illustrations, columns, different font types, sizes and colours, etc. When modifying materials for pupils with visual impairment, the original content should be considered in addition to layout to produce equivalent accessible materials.

The accompanying CD contains examples that illustrate some ways materials can be modified, with particular reference to content rather than layout. These examples use the approaches described below to modify the original material to meet the needs of pupils with visual impairment. These examples are presented in large print format; however, braille materials can also be produced using these approaches. All pupils have individual needs, so different approaches may be needed with different pupils; these examples should be viewed as suggestions only.

The first step is to determine the learning aims and the purpose of any diagrams and illustrative material; teachers and support staff should work together to identify the information to be retained. Consider carefully the time needed to interpret diagrams; in many cases, the time needed to interpret a diagram may outweigh the advantages of producing a diagram.

Removing non-essential illustrations and diagrams completely

Many materials include illustrations, diagrams and complex layout simply to illustrate the text without adding any new information. In such cases, removing these visual stimuli should be sufficient to enable access to the question. (examples 1 and 2)

Modifying illustrations and diagrams to reduce visual demand

In many cases, complex illustrations and diagrams can be simplified to reduce the visual demand. Examples include replacing drawings with simple symbols (example 3), presenting only the essential part of a diagram (example 4), simplifying a pattern (example 5), changing the orientation of a diagram (example 6) and replacing an illustration with a table (example 7).

Here are some essential features of accessible illustrations and diagrams:

- unnecessary clutter removed
- three-dimensional perspective removed
- bold symbols, patterns, textures and lines
- solid shading for print diagrams
- keys in place of labels, which may clutter the diagram and obscure content
- diagrams should be large enough to allow clear separation between different areas but small enough to enable pupils to access the whole diagram (e.g. the size of a two-hand span for tactile diagrams, no larger than A4 for a print diagram).

When modifying diagrams and illustrations, it is important to remember that pupils with visual impairment can often only see or feel small sections of a diagram in detail at any one time and will need to mentally piece the image together to create the whole. Pupils with visual impairment also find it difficult to interpret a large number of different symbols, patterns or textures on one diagram.

Replacing or supplementing illustrations and diagrams with written descriptions

Sometimes, it may be more appropriate to replace or supplement an illustration or diagram with a written description. The written description should give the user the information in the illustration or diagram. For some learning resource materials, it may be appropriate to give additional information to provide a context that may not be familiar to pupils with visual impairment. However, for assessment materials, be careful that the description does not give the answer to the question. (examples 8–12)

Replacing or supplementing illustrations and diagrams with real objects or models

Some materials involve illustrations or diagrams that can be readily presented as real objects or models. In many cases, real objects are more meaningful to pupils than print or tactile diagrams that present three-dimensional objects in two-dimensional representation. (examples 13 and 14)

Reducing the amount of information

Some materials require pupils to scan tables, graphs or text to obtain information. Scanning tasks involving locating specific information quickly and accurately present a much greater challenge for pupils with visual impairment. Enlarging diagrams can often make them too large for pupils to handle and scan, and, in many cases, too large to fit on a sheet of paper or thermoform plastic. Consider reducing the amount of information pupils need to scan through to find the information needed to complete the task. (examples 15–17)

Altering the measurements

Pupils with visual impairment should not be expected to measure and draw to the same degree of accuracy as sighted pupils. Generally, pupils should be expected to measure and draw to the nearest 5mm or 5° only. Materials may either be altered so that pupils measure and draw to the nearest 5mm or 5° only, or different tolerances may be applied when marking pupils' work. (example 18)

Amending the response method

Pupils are often required to complete tasks by drawing, creating or completing diagrams, charts and tables, etc. Pupils with visual impairment may find these tasks difficult and may require support staff to work as amanuenses. However, in many cases the task can be modified to enable pupils to complete their work independently. (examples 1, 3, 5, 8–11, 19)

Replacing inherently visual material with equivalent non-visual material

Some materials rely on visual contexts in such a way that pupils with visual impairment may be unable to access the material. For example, pupils may be asked to design an advertisement using visual images and layout. Pupils with visual impairment could be asked to design a radio advertisement to convey the same information, or create sound clips to insert into an advertisement created on a word processor or publishing software. In some cases, the task may be accessible to a pupil, but a visual context may confuse pupils. Removing the context may be sufficient to enable pupils to access the task. (example 20)

Resources

- The RNIB publication *Well Prepared* (RNIB 2001) is a guide to how examination and assessment materials are modified.

- Examples of modified large print and braille materials are available from examinations boards. In England, past national curriculum tests in modified formats are available from the National Assessment Agency.

4.6 Moon

Moon is an alternative reading method to braille. Moon is primarily used by people with visual impairment and additional difficulties, such as learning difficulties or poor finger sensitivity. Moon is based on the shapes of the letters in the written alphabet making it a less complicated reading system than braille. However, the disadvantage of Moon is that it takes more space than grade 1 braille and materials can be difficult to obtain.

Figure 4.4

Moon uses lines and curves to create 9 basic shapes; rotating or reflecting these shapes in different ways creates the 26 letters of the alphabet. These 26 characters, along with some punctuation marks and a numeral sign, complete grade 1 Moon. Grade 2 Moon is also available, which uses some additional signs and a simple form of shorthand; for example the word 'yesterday' is represented by 'yd'.

There are two methods for producing Moon: traditional Moon, which is printed on heat swell paper with solid raised lines, and dotted (or 'dotty') Moon, which is printed on a braille embosser with shapes made of braille dots.

Resources

- For more information on Moon, including a Moon font and how to obtain Moon resources, visit the Moon Literacy website (www.moonliteracy.org.uk).

- Children's books in Moon are available to loan from ClearVision (www.clearvisionproject.org).

4.7 Audio

Many pupils with visual impairment use audio as a simple and effective medium for accessing information. Careful consideration should be given to the nature of the material to be recorded. Materials containing diagrams and tables may be difficult to explain in audio format. Audio presentation is most appropriate for presenting large chunks of text, e.g. novels, plays and factual books.

Audio cassettes and compact discs

Producing recorded material on cassette or CD is relatively straightforward and does not require expensive specialist equipment. Cassettes are simple to create and easily accessible; however, cassettes may not be appropriate where pupils are required to locate specific information or in the classroom where pupils may become socially isolated. Audio presentation is likely to be most beneficial for background reading at home. CDs and digital audio may be more accessible as information can be recorded in sections making it easier to navigate.

Pupils may find audio useful for presenting work to teachers, particularly for braille users, avoiding the need to transcribe work for marking.

DAISY books

DAISY stands for Digital Accessible Information System. A DAISY book is a digital audio book that allows the user to navigate it as a print user would navigate a print book. DAISY books can be read using a DAISY Talking Book player or DAISY software on a computer. A DAISY player is similar to a CD player, enabling the user to access tracks quickly. There are a range of DAISY players with different features, such as adding bookmarks and footnotes, and the ability to jump from chapter to chapter, heading to heading and page to page.

Resources

- Audio books in DAISY format are available to loan from RNIB's Talking Books Library Service (www.rnib.org.uk/talkingbooks).

- Audio books in CD and cassette format are available to loan from Listening Books (www.listening-books.org.uk) and from Calibre (www.calibre.org.uk).

- Audio books can be purchased from a number of places, including the Talking Book shop (www.talkingbooks.co.uk).

- Audio newspapers and magazines are available in a choice of formats, including cassette, CD and email, from the Talking Newspaper Association of the UK (www.tnauk.org.uk). For information on local talking newspapers, visit the Talking News Federation website (www.tnf.org.uk).

- For information on DAISY books and DAISY players, visit www.daisy.org

- The BookCourier is a portable player designed for people with visual impairment for listening to electronic text, digital files and music. It is available from AccessABLE World (www.accessableworld.co.uk) and Techno-Vision Systems Ltd (www.techno-vision.co.uk).

- For information on accessing computers using audio, see 4.10 Access technology.

4.8 Visual displays

Visual displays are an integral part of the school environment, exhibiting pupils' work and providing visual stimulation. With some careful planning, visual displays can be made accessible for pupils with a range of visual impairments.

- Display pupils' work, and other display materials, at an appropriate height; this will vary according to the nature of the visual impairment, but is likely to be at arm's reach for pupils who use braille and at eye level for pupils who can access print.

- Use large and clear print.

- Mount displays on a clearly contrasting background. Avoid placing print over coloured or busy backgrounds.

- Avoid smooth, laminated and shiny materials to reduce glare.

- Provide tactile displays with braille labels at the correct height for pupils to feel. Clear plastic braille labels are useful as they do not obscure the background.

- If visual displays are used to promote important health and safety information, consider how this information is to be conveyed to, and retained by, pupils with visual impairment.

- If possible and appropriate, include some three-dimensional 'real' artefacts in the display which can be handled by pupils.

- If a wall display is introduced or changed, ensure that pupils with visual impairment are told about this so that they may take the opportunity to go and examine the display. Encourage full and honest feedback from all pupils to ensure continuous improvement.

- Provide a folder with individual copies of posters such as word lists, mathematical formulae, etc., to enable pupils with visual impairment to access information that is easily available in the classroom to sighted pupils.

4.9 Copyright and accessible copies

The Copyright (Visually Impaired Persons) Act 2002 amends the Copyright Designs and Patents Act 1988. The Act removes the need to obtain permission to produce accessible copies of published materials, including educational materials. The Act defines an accessible copy as 'a version which provides for a visually impaired person improved access to the work'. This includes braille, audio, accessible print and electronic versions.

The Act

The Act defines a 'visually impaired person' as a person:

- a) who is blind;
- b) who has an impairment of visual function that cannot be improved, by the use of corrective lenses, to a level that would normally be acceptable for reading without a special level or kind of light;

c) who is unable, through physical disability, to hold or manipulate a book; or

d) who is unable, through physical disability, to focus or move his eyes to the extent that would normally be acceptable for reading.

Accessible copies

A single accessible copy may be made of any printed material for a person with visual impairment so long as the original print copy accompanies it. The accessible version can be shared with others, but the original print copy must remain with it at all times so that only one person can read the material at any one time.

All accessible copies must contain acknowledgement of the source, including title, author and edition. The accessible copy must also contain wording to indicate that it has been created under the terms of Section 31A of the Copyright, Designs and Patents Act 1988 as amended by the Copyright (Visually Impaired Persons) Act 2002.

Restrictions

The right to produce an accessible copy does NOT apply if an equivalent accessible copy is already available commercially. To check if an equivalent accessible copy is available commercially, try contacting the publisher of the material and other sources such as Revealweb or the RNIB National Library.

More information

Licensing schemes are available for educational establishments wishing to make multiple copies of published material. For more information contact:

- Copyright Licensing Agency, 90 Tottenham Court Road, London, WIP 4LP. Tel: 020 7436 5931; fax: 020 7436 3986; email: cla@cla.co.uk

For information on producing multiple accessible copies of sheet music, contact:

- Music Publishers Association, 3rd Floor, Strandgate, 18/20 York Buildings, London, WC2N 6JU. Tel: 020 7839 7779; fax 020 7839 7776; email: info@mpaonline.org.uk

For more information on the Act, contact RNIB, the Copyright Licensing Agency, the Music Publishers Association or the UK Patent Office (The Patent Office, Concept House, Cardiff Road, Newport, NP10 8QQ. Tel: 01633 814000; fax: 01633 813600; email: enquiries@patent.gov.uk).

Adapted from RNIB's factsheet: 'Accessible Information: Copyright (Visually Impaired Persons) Act 2002'.

4.10 Access technology

Access technology encompasses a range of equipment that enables people with visual impairment to interact with technology. The terms 'adaptive technology', 'assistive technology' and 'enabling technology' also refer to methods for people with visual impairment to access computers. Access technology includes:

- adaptive hardware or software to make equipment accessible
- equipment specifically designed for use by people with visual impairment
- the role technology can play in accessing information or completing tasks.

Screen magnifier software

Screen magnifier software zooms in on the computer screen detail, making it big enough to see, so that users can read text without straining their eyes or adopting a poor seating posture. Colours, contrast and brightness can be altered to suit individual needs.

Video magnifiers

Video magnifiers, or closed circuit televisions (CCTVs), produce large text on a screen using a small camera connected to a computer monitor or television screen. Video magnifiers are mostly used for reading, but can also be used for writing and tasks such as sewing.

A variety of video magnifiers are available. Desktop models have a monitor with a camera that points downwards at the object to be viewed. Printed material and objects are placed on a platform under the camera and the image appears on the screen. Magnification, contrast and colour can be adapted for individual needs.

One of the cheapest video magnifiers is the kind that can plug into a television set or monitor; this can be a camera unit that looks like a large computer mouse or

Figure 4.5 Video magnifier © RNIB

a camera connected to a stand. There are also video magnifiers that can share a monitor with a computer, enabling users to work with the computer and paper material at the same time, and video magnifiers that can focus on a distant object, such as a whiteboard.

A wide range of portable units are also available. Some have a small screen built in; others have viewing goggles and camera unit linked by cable.

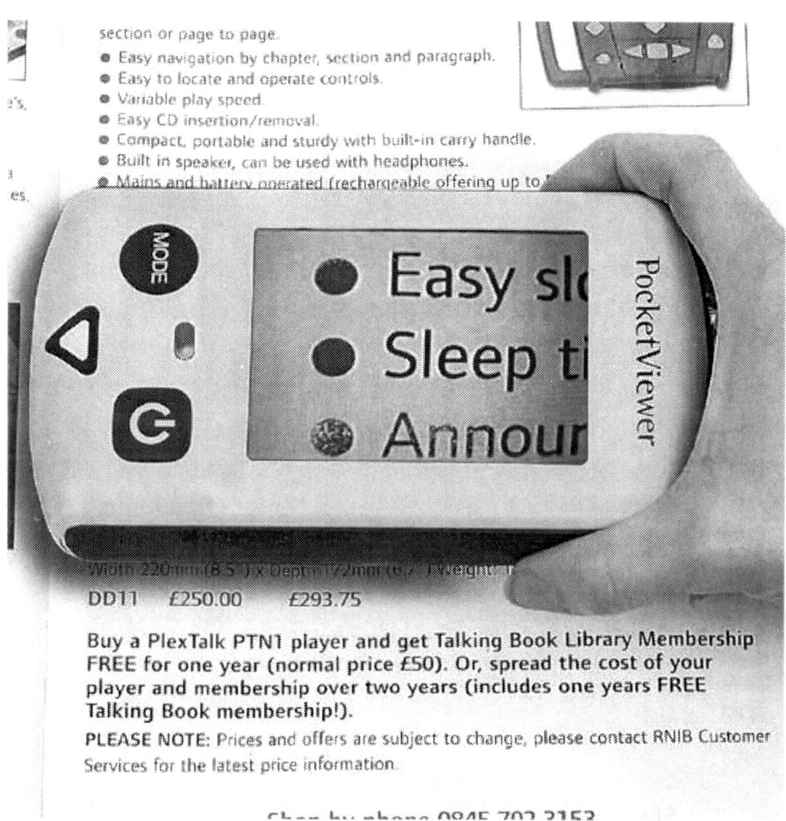

Figure 4.6   Video magnifier © RNIB

Screen reader software

Pupils who are unable to access computer output visually may benefit from speech output. Screen reader software speaks text aloud, in a synthesised voice, through computer speakers. The user listens to the output, wearing headphones when appropriate. Users navigate the screen and control the voice with the keyboard. Examples of screen readers include JAWS for screen reading and Supernova for both screen reading and enlarging. Screen readers are compatible with commonly used software and include shortcut keys. Most screen readers are compatible with screen magnifier software.

Scanners

Scanners use optical character recognition (OCR) software to turn printed text into digital text, which can be magnified or read by a screen reader. In their simplest form, handouts, magazine articles and books are placed face down under a hinged lid. At the press of a button, the scanner reads the text out loud. A few basic controls allow the user to review passages. Scanners may be stand-alone units or an add-on to a computer. Scanners are probably most useful in a central location such as a library or resource base, where pupils need to do large amounts of research.

Braille displays

Braille displays are lightweight electro-mechanical devices that protrude from underneath the front of a standard computer keyboard. The device presents the information on screen as braille, a line at a time. Each cell on the display is controlled electronically and consists of pins that move up and down to produce braille output. Braille displays can be used independently or with a screen reader. Braille displays are especially useful for those who have both visual and hearing impairments.

Braille notetakers

Braille notetakers are portable, bespoke devices, about the size of a hardback book. The braille keyboard contains a key for each of the six braille dots and a space bar, so that the braille code can be used when typing. Text can be entered, edited, read back via speech or braille and printed in braille or ink. The latest machines can connect to computer networks and perform all the functions found in any personal digital organiser (PDA). Some have internal microphones, enabling them to act like digital audiotape machines, which is useful for teaching foreign language pronunciation, or recording the results of an experiment. They can also connect to wireless computer networks for internet and email. The simplest way to get printed text from a braille notetaker is to use its infrared port to link to a suitably equipped local printer.

Figure 4.7   Braille notetaker © RNIB

Fatigue

Listening to screen readers, looking at magnified screens and reading braille are tiring activities, both physically and mentally. Pupils using access technology may need more frequent breaks and physical exercise to relieve muscle tension and restore concentration.

Resources

- The local authority sensory support service should be the first point of contact for queries regarding equipment and resources. Support services have resource bases of equipment and materials and may contact other organisations on your behalf if further help is needed.
- See 18.1 Directory of suppliers for access technology suppliers.

CHAPTER 5

Assessment

5.1 Formal assessment

Assessment is an integral part of the whole-school curriculum, which contributes to the learning and achievements of all pupils. Pupils' approaches to learning can be influenced by the nature of assessment; therefore assessment methods should be chosen that enable all pupils to demonstrate their learning achievements. All staff and pupils involved should understand the purpose of the assessment, e.g. to monitor learning, assess attainment, provide feedback to staff, pupils and parents.

Modifying assessments

Modification of assessments for pupils with visual impairment should follow the same principles as modification of classroom materials. Modifications should enable pupils to access the assessment without causing unfair advantage or disadvantage. Support staff should work closely with teachers to understand assessment objectives and provide accessible assessment materials.

Adult support

Pupils with visual impairment may require adult support for activities they are unable to take part in independently. Readers and amanuenses should be considered for pupils who have difficulty reading and/or writing for sustained periods of time. Pupils with visual impairment may also require assistance with practical activities, such as using equipment, locating materials, drawing, measuring, etc.

Recording results

It is important to distinguish between learning achievements and the ability to record results. For example, in mathematics pupils may be required to draw a bar chart to represent the data in a table. The objective is to assess pupils' ability to interpret data and represent the data using a different format, not to assess pupils' ability to draw. Pupils with visual impairment who experience difficulties drawing may not be able to demonstrate their understanding through drawing a bar chart but may be able to direct an adult, working as an amanuensis, to complete the bar chart for them or alternatively they may be able to produce a written description of the bar chart. Similarly, a pupil learning braille may not yet have the braille skills to complete a piece of creative writing incorporating full punctuation and layout, but may be able to demonstrate their creative writing abilities by producing an audio recording.

Time allowances

Pupils with visual impairment often require additional time to process visual information and complete written and practical tasks. Many external examinations recognise this requirement and many allow up to 100 per cent additional time for pupils with visual impairment. Teachers should consider the nature of the assessment and the purpose of time restrictions.

Alternative methods of assessment

In some instances, formal assessment methods may not be appropriate for pupils with visual impairment. For example, pupils with visual impairment may find it difficult to read for long periods of time or may be unable to access some parts of the curriculum, e.g. 'sight-reading' music. Teachers should consider using non-formal methods of assessment, such as classroom work, where a pupil's attainment in a formal assessment situation does not reflect ability or attainment in the classroom.

External assessment

For most external assessments, modified versions of tests and examination materials are available, in addition to a range of access arrangements (formerly known as special arrangements). Modified formats, order processes and access arrangements vary depending on the country, age group and awarding or regulatory body.

In England, modified versions of the national curriculum statutory tests and optional test materials are available for Key Stages 1, 2 and 3 and can be ordered from the National Assessment Agency (NAA). Information about access arrangements, such as early opening for adaptations, readers, amanuenses, etc., can be found on the NAA website (www.naa.org.uk/tests). Schools receive information about how to order modified tests, how to make access arrangement applications and how to obtain past papers for familiarisation purposes early in the autumn. These processes can change from year to year, as can deadlines for ordering, so it is important to think about modified test requirements early in the academic year.

For formal qualifications, the Joint Council for Qualifications (JCQ) represents awarding bodies from across the UK. Regulations and application forms for access arrangements are common to all awarding bodies; however, schools need to make separate applications to each awarding body.

Resources

- The NAA website (www.naa.org.uk/tests) has information about national curriculum tests in England.

- To obtain copies of past modified statutory national curriculum tests in England, contact the Modified Test Agency (Statutory) on 0870 321 6727 or email helpline@pia.co.uk.

- To obtain copies of past modified optional tests in England for years 3, 4, 5, 7, 8 and the year 7 progress test, contact the Modified Test Agency (Optional) on 01733 375356 or email qca@rnib.org.uk.

- Information about access arrangements for general qualifications is available on the JCQ website (www.jcq.org.uk), and is updated every September.

- 'GCE, VCE, GCSE and GNVQ examinations – specification for the preparation and production of examination papers for candidates with a visual impairment' provides detailed guidance about how examination papers are modified and produced in braille and modified large print, including information on fonts, enlarged simplified and tactile diagrams, and some subject-specific information too. This document is available on RNIB's website (www.rnib.org.uk/curriculum).

- To obtain copies of past modified examination papers, contact the individual examination board. If past copies are not available, it might be worth placing a request on the online BECTA VI Forum to see if another school or support service has a spare copy (http://lists.becta.org.uk/mailman/listinfo/vi-forum).

5.2 Informal assessment

Informal assessment allows pupils to demonstrate their knowledge in situations that are more familiar and comfortable to them. The assessment is formative; its aim is to aid the learning process. This in turn should help pupils move forward in their learning. In many situations it can be argued that pupils are continually assessed informally, every day, indeed minute-by-minute.

Informal assessment might include:

- observational reports from teachers and parents

- structured collation and analysis of work samples from pupils

- specifically tailored teacher tests.

The specialist teacher for visual impairment has an important role in providing day-to-day access to the curriculum, by modifying, enlarging or transcribing materials as appropriate and, as important, providing the correct feedback to class/subject teachers and parents.

It is vital that the specialist teacher, class teacher and subject teachers work closely together as a team throughout the academic year. The specialist teacher should be well informed about the teaching objectives and also the learning outcomes for a particular subject. With such close collaboration, the aims and outcomes of everyday assessment should follow easily. Take care to remember that the needs and learning strategies of pupils with visual impairment are as varied as those of sighted pupils, i.e. this is not a 'one rule fits all' situation.

In many cases, informal assessment is a more effective diagnostic tool than formal assessment for pupils with visual impairment. Formal assessments, even with modifications and allowances, do not always compensate for the effect that loss of vision will have on the outcome of the assessment, e.g. allowing additional time to complete a test does not properly address the concept of visual fatigue.

5.3 Assessment of functional vision

There are many different levels of visual impairment. The level of impairment and the use that a pupil makes of their residual vision will determine the pupil's requirements.

All pupils with visual impairment require a functional vision assessment. A specialist teacher for visual impairment assesses how pupils use residual vision within the educational and classroom environment. A written report will ensure that each pupil's visual needs are identified and provided for. This provides teaching and support staff with the information required to ensure pupils access appropriate equipment, specific curriculum needs are provided for and any additional support is given.

Main aims of assessing functional vision

The main aims of assessing functional vision are to:

- provide continuity of provision for pupils' needs
- assist staff in planning and developing the curriculum
- assist staff in ensuring that a fully modified and differentiated curriculum is provided
- set realistic targets for pupils
- suggest any adaptations in teaching approaches
- ensure that pupils have full curriculum entitlement alongside fully-sighted peers
- detail specific equipment that pupils may require to access the curriculum.

Key areas for assessment

The following areas of functional vision are assessed:

- near vision
- distance vision
- depth perception
- peripheral vision
- colour vision.

The assessment determines pupils':

- preferred lighting
- preferred format for presentation of materials, e.g. photocopy enlargement, modified large print, braille, audio
- preferred print size, font type and use of contrast
- preferred text, paper and illustration colours
- preferred type and colour of writing implements
- preferred use of OHPs, whiteboard, blackboard, TV
- preferred contrast of text on computer screens, e.g. black on white, white on black, enlargement of icons
- equipment requirements, e.g. sloping desk, magnifiers, laptop, coloured papers, large print calculators, audio recording equipment
- preferred seating position within the classroom and the seating position for support staff where required.

The report will also conclude with recommendations regarding formal mobility assessment, safety implications within the school environment, additional learning support and external assessment.

Conclusion

A summary of advice and a recommendation sheet should accompany the full and detailed visual assessment report. The report will also be essential in the preparation of an IEP (see 3.4 Individual education plans).

Subject-specific issues

CHAPTER 6

Art and design

6.1 Teaching art

Painting is a blind man's profession. He paints, not what he sees, but what he feels, what he tells himself about what he has seen.

(Picasso)

Art encourages pupils to explore their environment through visual, aural and tactile methods. Art helps develop communication, visual skills, aural skills, tactile skills, fine motor skills, self-discipline and can boost confidence and self-esteem. Many well-known artists were visually impaired, including Monet, Degas and Renoir. Visual impairment should not be considered a barrier to art education. Pupils' different views and experiences of the world around them should be explored and embraced.

Art and pupils with visual impairment

Modify teaching strategies to reflect pupils' visual, auditory and tactile abilities. Pupils with severe visual impairment often experience only what is within arm's reach and can be safely touched or directly heard. Develop pupils' observational skills and encourage pupils to use both visual and tactile abilities to full potential.

Forming concepts of large objects and relationships between objects is often difficult; small models may help pupils better understand scale, space and form. The process of exploration may be a more important learning experience for pupils than the resulting piece of artwork.

Teaching strategies

- Many pupils with visual impairment have not had the range of visual experiences available to their sighted peers. It is important to provide first-hand experiences and aids to learning. Visits to museums, galleries and other places of interest help develop observation skills and understanding of the visual and tactile world. Many museums and galleries provide audio description and some offer tours specifically for people with visual impairment.

- Do not assume prior knowledge – even simple directions such as 'above', 'on top of' and 'over' may need to be clarified.

- Supplement visual demonstrations with spoken communication and instructions. Choose your words carefully and make your instructions clear.

- Encourage pupils to consider their own ideas by making choices and decisions about their work. This can be done through questions and class discussion.

- Encourage pupils to discuss their own and each other's work.

- Encourage pupils to explore different methods and materials and to choose methods and materials suited to their own needs.

- Encourage pupils to be realistic about what they can and cannot do, and be realistic in your own expectations.

- Allow pupils to make mistakes without criticism, but use these incidents as a discussion point. 'Happy accidents' can make attractive artwork!

- Allow pupils to work out which part of the task they can complete and which part will require assistance. Negotiate who does what; no matter how tedious or time-consuming, allow pupils to perform their chosen tasks. Supporting adults should not complete pupils' work without their permission. Pupils with visual impairment often have a very accurate tactile memory for their work and can feel upset if their pieces have been altered.

- Most important – have fun!

Resources

- i-Map (www.tate.org.uk/imap) is an award-winning arts resource from Tate Online that is aimed at people with visual impairment with a general interest in art as well as teachers and pupils with visual impairment.

- The Living Paintings Trust (www.livingpaintings.org) provides a free library service for people with visual impairment of all ages, enabling access to albums of art collections. Each album contains raised images, audio descriptions and colour reproductions of at least 10 works of art. The collections are designed to group together topics in an interesting and exciting way.

6.2 Drawing

Drawing is not a matter of what you can see, it's a question of what you can make other people see.

(Degas)

We tend to think of drawing as a purely visual art form, thus making it inaccessible for anyone with severe visual impairment. However, thinking more broadly, it is possible even for someone with no sight to reproduce an image on a two-dimensional surface.

Tactile drawing

Rebecca Harris, a successful young artist with whom the author has worked (she achieved a first class honours degree in fine arts and is now working professionally), used masking tape, cut into narrow strips by support staff, to produce her drawings. Masking tape has the advantage of being moveable. She would explore the subject with her hands – yes, even the life model, which caused some hilarity – and then gradually build up the image. As with using the eyes to study the subject, she had to keep referring back with her hands as she checked each detail. The result may not have been visually accurate but it was certainly a successful tactile representation. For more details and examples of Rebecca's work, visit www.rebeccaharris.org.uk.

Figure 6.1 Positive and negative me
These are a series of tactile pictures exploring the different shapes that can be made by the body with the use of positive and negative space. In the tactile version of these pictures (produced on heat swell paper), the black is raised from the page (the positive) and the white is not raised (the negative).
© Rebecca Harris

Other suitable materials for producing tactile drawings include pipe cleaners, Wikki Stix and strips of other tactile materials such as sandpaper and ribbon. Tacti Mark is a liquid plastic that dries to produce raised, high visibility and permanent shapes; available in fluorescent orange, black and white. Drawing film is ideal for producing quick tactile images; simply draw on it with a stylus or ballpoint pen to produce a raised line. The options are limited only by your imagination!

Drawing for pupils using print

The approach used depends very much on the type and degree of visual loss. Some pupils may need to handle real objects to produce an image. Pupils with moderate to severe visual impairment may find it difficult to produce drawings of large objects and landscapes that are unfamiliar to them, and often have difficulty with perspective. Experiment with different media, pencil lines may be too faint for many pupils. Using a drawing programme on the computer for initial drafts may be helpful as this can produce a far darker line, which can be modified before printing it out and then developing the idea.

Drawing for young children

Young children usually love to make marks on paper and most children with visual impairment are no exception. Provide a wide variety of media and background papers that contrast well so that the results can be clearly seen.

Points to remember

Some pupils with visual impairment may have incomplete concepts of the world around them. If they have to move close to an object to see it clearly, they may never be able to get the overall impression. It may help to provide a simple picture or photograph as a starting point if an overall image of something usually viewed from a distance is required.

Resources

- Wikki Stix, Tacti Mark and drawing film are all available from RNIB (www.rnib.org.uk).
- RNIB's book *Painting from a New Perspective* (2001) focuses on six artists who have continued painting after losing their sight. It describes, in practical terms, how and why these artists continued painting.
- The 'Painting and sight loss' section of RNIB's website has information on artists with visual impairment and links to other useful websites (www.rnib.org.uk/painting).

6.3 Modelling

Clay

It is important to develop the capacity to invent, create, interpret, make and evaluate. Many children with visual impairment are not encouraged to use crayons, felt pens, etc. to draw and colour like their sighted peers. It is important for pupils with visual impairment to experience similar creative processes, and models can be successful alternatives.

Clay is a versatile teaching tool and an extremely tactile material. It provides many of the tactile and sensory experiences that allow pupils to participate in creative activities. Clay modelling can be used to:

- encourage different movements or actions
- develop the sense of touch
- learn a new process or procedure
- help experience a sense of achievement by completing a task
- help achieve a sense of accomplishment and independence.

Although specialist equipment is needed to glaze and fire finished artefacts made from clay, it is important to understand that the process of clay modelling is more important than the final product. If clay sculptures are allowed to air dry over a period of time they will always remain fragile and water permeable, but they can be painted and varnished as finished examples of the process. If you have access to a kiln, teach pupils how clay is fired and encourage safe handling.

Teach simple techniques such as thumb pots (pinch pots), which are shaped in both hands using small balls of clay. This is an ideal technique as it relies on touch to feel thickness and consistency of shape. Techniques such as coil pots and slab construction can also be taught. Try different types of decoration by indenting lines or shapes and add patterns by applying pieces of clay either at random or to form a repeating pattern. Demonstrate each process and allow pupils to feel and try for themselves. An interesting experiment is to give a group of pupils a Chinese spoon and bowl and ask them to recreate these items in clay – without instruction.

Be careful to distinguish between lack of skill and lack of vision. Some pupils will never progress beyond following instructions and some will develop their work with genuine curiosity and creativity.

When pupils are first introduced to clay it is important to establish a tactile vocabulary. Encourage pupils to record their first impressions, e.g. cold, damp, moist, soft, smelly, etc. Ask questions and encourage discussion. As clay is worked by warm hands discuss the fact that it becomes drier and less malleable. Clay that is to be modelled over several sessions must be kept moist with damp paper towels or newspaper, sealed in polythene and stored in a cool place. Pupils need to understand the importance of this procedure. Ask questions that will allow pupils to begin understanding the characteristics of clay and the process of creating pottery.

Many pupils with visual impairment do not recognise or value their own work after it has been fired, as it feels significantly different to touch. Any small imperfections that have not been smoothed out when the clay was soft will feel brittle and sharp and the actual piece of clay work can shrink by as much as a third in size. Ensure pupils know about these changes and understand why they happen.

In all modelling work it is essential to provide a point of reference. Do not assume prior knowledge, e.g. some pupils with visual impairment will talk about a bird's mouth and not know from first-hand experience that it has a beak or what shape it is. A fun first lesson using clay is to make sausage, fried egg and beans all using different rolling processes. Do your research first – pupils may have eaten these foods but may never have held them in their hands.

Clay alternatives

For those without access to a kiln and pottery facilities, there are several brands of modelling materials and synthetic clays such as Newclay, which can be bought at art supply outlets. Newclay is a reinforced air-drying modelling clay that can be painted and treated with varnish to give a long-lasting final product. It does not provide the range of tactile experiences that pot clay provides, but it is excellent for smaller projects and is less messy.

Papier mâché

Papier mâché is a cheap and effective way of making three-dimensional works and relief models. It is made by using paper and paste that is either pulped or layered onto a base. Any kind of paper can be used, newspapers are cheap and effective, but it is worth experimenting with different types of paper for different effects. Cellulose paste can be bought from most art supply catalogues and is preferable to wallpaper paste, which contains fungicide. Recipes for mixing paste from flour and water can be found on the internet and in good craft books. Ready-made paper pulp can also be bought and mixed with water; it can be modelled like clay and painted and varnished when hard.

Models can be made by preparing an initial shape, skeleton, wire armature or outline depending on the materials at hand. Construction of the initial shape should involve some research and problem solving.

- Investigate examples, e.g. fish – real fish, models, cartoons, ornaments and tiles; discuss shapes and markings.

- Look at a range of junk and materials – plastic bottles, cardboard, chicken wire, balloons. Which shape most closely resembles the examples? Can these be adapted: bottles cut, cans squashed or cardboard shaped?

- Decide on the best shapes and use as a basic skeleton onto which papier mâché will be applied.

- Consider how the work will be displayed and incorporate this into the design.

Pupils can prepare the paper by tearing it into small pieces, initially about the size of half a five-pound note. You may need to demonstrate this size or give a recognisable alternative. After they have prepared their paper, these pieces can be applied to the basic shape with paste and smoothed on by hand. It is a good idea to try and cover as much as possible in one session as this makes subsequent work easier. At least three layers can give a hard wooden texture. Too much paste makes the model difficult to handle and too little means that the paper does not adhere to the surface easily and will flake off as it dries. It is a very tactile process and requires good manual dexterity to manage all the activities together.

The recycled materials are cheap and versatile and allow quite sizeable constructions depending on the skeleton. It is best to start with a small item such as a bowl or mask to establish the technique before trying larger projects. Papier mâché modelling lends itself to working in stages in a school environment and provides a material that is non-toxic, easily handled and limited only by the imagination.

For recipes, ideas and techniques for papier mâché, visit www.papiermache.co.uk

6.4 Colour

Some pupils may not have colour vision or may have types of colour blindness. Those who have lost their sight may retain a visual memory; others may have no memory of colour at all. For pupils with no light or colour perception, no amount of tactile exploration can reveal information about colour. Pupils with visual impairment need to build on their knowledge and comprehension of the world and this includes some understanding of colour and its concepts.

Colour by association

Most colour concepts are formed through discussion and conversation, but some must be memorised. Specifics like primary, secondary and tertiary colours can be taught but may seem meaningless if they are just words without visual impact.

Encourage pupils to learn colour vocabulary through songs such as 'I can sing a rainbow': 'Red and yellow and pink and green, purple and orange and blue'.

Colour can be chosen by association, e.g. traditional Christmas colours are mostly red, green and gold, derived from holly and Christmas trees. Pupils could choose colours associated with their favourite football team. Colour by association can be a personal experience and may be different for each pupil.

Use of senses

We can use other senses to describe colours; warm colours like the yellow from the sun or fiery red, icy white and cool blue. Sour lemon (yellow), red hot chilli (red) and cool cucumber (green) are all associated with taste. Colour can be communicated even if it cannot be seen. This verse from a poem by Roger McGough demonstrates how descriptions need not be visual:

> The sun has a custardy flavour
> And the clouds are as light as air,
> The wind with a chewier texture,
> With a hint of cinnamon there?

Encourage discussion

Artwork can help to educate by considering both the real and imagined world. Conversations and discussions, which help to promote individual perceptions through building up a vocabulary including descriptions of colours, can take place any time, any where.

There are many gaps in the knowledge of pupils with visual impairment and the best way to understand their invisible environment and contribute to their understanding of our highly visual world is through conversation. The questions they ask are not always the ones you might expect and are difficult to answer: 'What colour is the wind?' requires a bit of imagination.

Some pupils will believe that colour has no relevance or interest; just as many sighted people have little interest in colour and its variations. Others will become aware of colour codes perhaps in fashion or details of their environment and these will become their rules. The sea and sky will always be blue; grass and trees will always be green.

Resources

- Scented marker pens, available from RNIB and art suppliers, help pupils choose colours for drawing.

- Scented colour papers are available from Zychem Ltd (www.zychem.co.uk).

- Tactile colour packs, available from The Sensory Company (www.thesensorycompany.co.uk), consist of different coloured paper with individual textures designed for each colour.

CHAPTER 7

Design and technology

7.1 Marking and measuring

Accurate marking and measuring can make the difference between success and failure in many areas of design and technology. Standard methods may be difficult for pupils with visual impairment as they often rely on small or faint detail. However, there are alternatives that can enable a good degree of independence.

Increasing visibility in the classroom

- Highlight the main markings on measuring containers such as jugs and weighing scales in a strong colour.
- Use a contrasting colour when marking a line, e.g. for cutting along. Stick a length of masking or insulating tape along the edge of the cutting line to avoid marking the end product.
- Use contrasting containers and ensure that equipment contrasts well against the working surface.
- Good lighting, particularly focused on the work, is essential.
- Encourage pupils to use low vision aids, be they simple magnifiers or sophisticated video magnifiers. Efficient use can enable a far greater degree of independence (see 4.10 Access technology).
- If pupils have the opportunity to explore and use equipment away from the pressure of the lesson situation, they are likely to be far more confident and may also be able to identify difficulties and suggest possible strategies to overcome them, and make the task more accessible.

Resources

- Tactile rulers and angle measurers are available from RNIB (see 12.4 Drawing and measuring).
- For measuring liquids, liquid level indicators are available from a number of suppliers (see 18.1 Directory of suppliers).

7.2 Textiles – Stitching and sewing

Sewing is a task that many people think of as being very visual and, therefore, not suitable for anyone with a visual impairment. However, tactile skill is necessary for stitching and enables pupils with visual impairment to experience this craft.

Choice of materials

- For beginners, any material with clearly defined holes is helpful. This does not even have to be fabric. Plastic canvas is an excellent starting point and the basic stitching movement can be mastered using coloured laces. Binca and other open-weave fabrics are the logical progression. Once the basic process has been learnt, more varied materials may be introduced.

- Fairly thick threads, which do not fray easily, are better for beginners. More experienced pupils may progress to much finer materials.

- It may be helpful to stretch the fabric in an embroidery frame and to clamp this in a suitable position for work.

The importance of contrast

- For pupils with visual impairment, good contrast can make all the difference. Early experiences with needle and thread should be planned with this in mind.

- Contrast and visibility are further enhanced by good, glare-free, local lighting.

Threading the needle

Easy threading needles are now readily available. They have a latch at the side of the eye and are threaded by sliding the thread down along the side of the eye until it drops into place and the latch closes.

Using a sewing machine

It is possible for pupils with little or no vision to master the safe use of a sewing machine, with time and patience. A needle guard (available from good sewing machine stockists) will prevent fingers getting under the needle. However, the real key is to allow pupils plenty of time to become familiar with the machine and its workings, without the pressure of having a task to complete.

Texture

For pupils with no vision, texture is vital. Don't be afraid to explore alternative, non-conventional materials such as raffia, strips of leather or ribbon, hairy string, etc. This could introduce variety for the whole class.

Review

Even those with little or no vision can be given the opportunity to explore the possibilities of stitching and sewing. They are likely to need more time to become proficient at the techniques, and may, in fact, decide that this is not their preferred medium, but it should not prevent them from having a try.

Resources

- Binca fabric and easy threading needles are available from good needlecraft suppliers.

- Needle guards are usually fitted to sewing machines, but can also be bought from machine suppliers.

7.3 Food technology – Equipment and utensils

Much equipment commonly used in a food technology kitchen is suitable for use by pupils with visual impairment, with little or no adaptation. There is also a wide range of specialist equipment available.

Low-tech ideas

- It is good practice to collect all equipment and ingredients before starting. This is particularly so for pupils with visual impairment. It is also useful to establish a regular layout of the equipment at the workstation.

- Store equipment and utensils in a logical and orderly fashion, keeping a constant location for each piece of equipment. Label cupboards and drawers with large clear labels, with the addition of braille labels if appropriate. Make braille labels by embossing onto sticky-backed plastic, then peel off the backing to position the label. If using braille labels, be consistent in their positioning; pupils need to know where to feel for them.

- Tacti Mark is a liquid plastic that when dabbed on, dries to produce raised permanent shapes, which are highly visible. This is useful for marking dials on cookers, etc. as well as the scales on measuring equipment (e.g. measuring jugs). It is available from RNIB in fluorescent orange, black and white.

- Mark the upper edge of the handles of knives to indicate the reverse of the cutting edge; bright red nail polish works well.

- When measuring clear liquids, hold a piece of contrasting paper or card behind the jug so that the level can be seen more clearly.

- Non-slip mats (available from a range of suppliers including Dycem, www.dycem.com) help to prevent equipment from slipping. They can also provide a well-contrasted background.

- Good contrast and lighting can greatly increase visibility. Use coloured boards or trays if it is difficult to see utensils against the work surface. Contrast mixing bowls with what is being mixed in them (e.g. a darker colour for mixing pastry). Lighting that shines directly onto the working area is helpful, so long as it does not produce glare. If necessary ask a specialist teacher for visual impairment about task lighting.

Higher-tech ideas

- Digital displays on scales, microwave cookers, etc. are usually easier to read than analogue markings.

- A liquid level indicator is a small device that hooks over the edge of a cup, jug or bowl and makes an audible sound when liquid touches it. This is far safer than testing with the finger, which is not advisable when using hot liquids.

- Liquid level indicators, talking measuring jugs, talking scales and talking microwave cookers are available from a range of suppliers (see 18.1 Directory of suppliers).

- Gas versus electric cookers: electric cookers are considered the safer option, as there are no naked flames. However, it is possible for pupils with visual impairment to use a gas cooker safely with careful instruction.

Review

There are many strategies to make it easier for pupils with visual impairment to take part in practical work in food technology and thus also learn valuable strategies for independent living. Maximising contrast and clarity will assist pupils with partial sight loss, whilst tactile learners will benefit from introducing texture as well as talking technology. Safe working should be explained and practised at all times. Some supervision may be desirable but should not prevent pupils from being as independent as possible.

7.4 Food technology – Modifying the task

It is easy to assume that a task that appears to rely on vision is impossible for pupils with visual impairment. However, by analysing exactly what the task is designed to achieve, there is often an alternative approach that will meet the same objective. The following examples illustrate how this might be done.

Looking at packaging

Task: study the details on an item of food packaging, analyse the content and then produce an example of packaging for a given food product. The instinct is often to approach the task from a visual point of view, concentrating on colour, layout and visual impact. Here is a real life example of how this task was approached by a pupil with visual impairment in the classroom.

- First, the example of packaging was opened out flat, so that its shape and the way it folded together could be studied.

- The opened packet was stuck onto card and all the main features given braille labels (e.g. product name, ingredients, weight, nutritional information, manufacturer). This would also work using large print.

- The features of packaging that were important to a blind user were discussed. One key feature that emerged was ease of opening.

- The pupil drew her design for a package using drawing film.

- A practical assistant supported the task of transferring the design to card and cutting it out.

- The pupil was then able to produce braille labels to stick onto the packaging to indicate the positions of the main features.

- The result, although not as visually pleasing as that of her peers, met the design criteria of being easy to open for someone with little or no vision.

Product comparisons

When comparing the results of a series of recipes for the same product, either manufactured or made by the pupils themselves, there is often an emphasis on visual presentation. However, visual appearance may be described to pupils with visual impairment. Pupils should be encouraged to compare non-visual features such as:

- taste
- smell
- texture
- ease of opening any packaging
- ease of eating (when you can't actually see what you are eating)
- preparation time and effort.

Review

Don't just think visual. We use all our senses to experience food, and exploring these possibilities can enrich the curriculum for the whole class.

CHAPTER 8

Geography

Geography is often considered one of the most difficult subjects for pupils with visual impairment. Many of the concepts involved are visual, such as large-scale distance and size, reading maps, visually descriptive language, etc. However, geography has much to offer for pupils with visual impairment who may have many gaps in their understanding of the environment in which we live and interact. Studying geography helps pupils learn about their surroundings and make sense of the world in which they live but are unable to see.

8.1 Basic plans

Using basic plans is probably the best way to start teaching pupils with visual impairment about maps. The technique described can also be used with older pupils with visual impairment who have not developed good spatial awareness. The main aim is for pupils to understand that a plan symbolises an aerial view of the area; by building a three-dimensional plan they can look or 'reach' down at it. It also teaches the use of symbols for representation. Here is a tried-and-tested method to make a basic plan.

Experience the area

Start by making a plan of an area that is already familiar to the pupil. Visit the area and make notes, by writing, brailling or recording audio. A dictation machine or portable audio player/recorder (e.g. MP3 player) is useful for this. Use the terms 'left' and 'right', or compass points, depending on the ability and knowledge of the pupil.

Build a three-dimensional plan

Listen to, or read back, the details of the area and from this start to build a three-dimensional plan. Useful building materials include: wooden or plastic blocks of various shapes and sizes, cardboard, modelling clay, Wikki Stix, sand, foam and commercial materials such as Lego or Duplo. Before starting, pupils can decide what each type of block will represent, e.g. cubes represent rooms, long narrow cuboids represent corridors, etc. These materials are also useful in the classroom for making instant models during lessons. Importantly, always build onto a baseboard, as you can guarantee that you will need to move the plan for some reason!

To reinforce spatial awareness and direction, use a small figure to move around the plan; this is often a difficult task for pupils with visual impairment.

Convert to two dimensions

When the three-dimensional plan is complete, pupils can copy it to create a two-dimensional version, using card of the same shape as the blocks. Stick the card shapes onto a piece of paper (double-sided tape works best for this). Pupils will probably need some support to align symbols. To make a permanent tactile record of the plan it can be copied onto thermoform plastic or swell paper. Labels can be put onto any of the plans at any stage.

Advanced plans

After pupils have built plans of familiar places, the same technique can be used to make plans of less familiar places, or larger-scale plans, e.g. the town centre. As pupils become more proficient they can make the symbols smaller, so that they can be felt under the fingertips. Pupils can also be encouraged to create their own symbols, perhaps incorporating texture as well as block shapes. If available, thermoform plastic can be used to create permanent copies of small three-dimensional plans. This technique will eventually lead to an understanding of more complex maps, including Ordnance Survey symbols.

Resources

Wikki Stix are available from RNIB (www.rnib.org.uk).

8.2 Accessible maps

Adapting original maps and providing outlines for pupils to record data are both vital skills to ensure access to the curriculum.

Key action points

- Use layers to build up a map rather than put too much information on one sheet, e.g. a map of leisure and tourism could become three maps of (a) physical features, (b) towns and communication links and (c) leisure facilities, with a key to each map.

- Simplify information and reduce clutter; consider reproducing only part of a map to give a focus. Be consistent with positioning of scale, title and key.

- Follow the original layout and colours of a map as far as possible as it will be easier for pupils to follow when reference is made to the information in follow-up sessions. Use clear bold fonts for labelling, e.g. 18 or 24 point in Arial. Use different patterns and textures for different parts of the map.

- Use technology, e.g. video magnifier or computer and scanner. If tracing an outline, use mouldable putty to attach overhead projector sheets or clear film to the screen and draw the key lines. Changing the background colour on screen may highlight information and make it clearer to follow. Download free outline maps from the internet rather than drawing or tracing them by hand.

- Prepare map outlines with a few key names, lines or features on which pupils can record data and more readily locate information with basic clues in place.

Resources

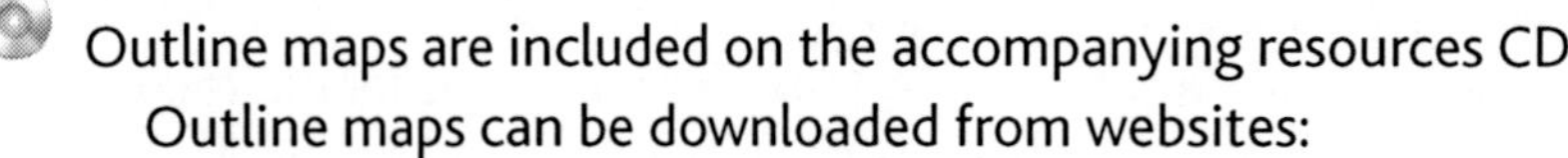

Outline maps are included on the accompanying resources CD.
Outline maps can be downloaded from websites:

- www.ordnancesurvey.co.uk has a 'get a map' feature with zoom and also a 'mapbuilder' programme with outlines and additional features and symbols, e.g. roads

- www.factmonster.com is an online atlas with maps and outlines

- www.mapsinminutes.com has editable worldwide political, satellite and relief maps

- Google Maps (http://maps.google.co.uk) is an online free map resource with uncluttered clear maps and satellite images with a zoom facility

- Google Earth (http://earth.google.com) is a broadband three-dimensional application with maps and satellite images; zoom from space to a local street.

Use access technology, e.g. video magnifier (preferably not a portable one as insufficient information can be shown on the screen at any time) and hand-held magnifiers for locating individual symbols or small details (see 4.10 Access technology).

8.3 Ordnance Survey maps

Ordnance Survey (OS) mapping skills are difficult for pupils with visual impairment. Realistically, only a very small number of people with visual impairment will ever need to access OS maps. However, they are now a compulsory requirement in some external geography examinations. In examination papers, the maps are modified to remove many of the distracting details but still require knowledge of basic symbols and an understanding of contours. Pupils are given an enlarged version of a small area of a map, with coordinates modified to four numbers.

Reading coordinates

Begin with basic grid games, progressing to two number coordinates, e.g. 'treasure hunts', 'find the coloured squares', 'alien attack'. Once the basics of reading coordinates are learnt, pupils can progress to modified maps. For these skills, black and white grids or raised line grids are easiest to follow.

Ordnance Survey symbols

To teach OS symbols, start with larger versions of the symbols, both in black and white and in colour. Play matching activities such as 'snap' with large print or tactile OS symbols.

Some tactile symbols are easy to follow, but others may not be as clear, as pupils will not be familiar with the corresponding visual symbol. In a study by Gardiner and Perkins (2003), pupils designed their own symbols, which bore little resemblance to the official OS symbols in some cases. Symbols need to be described orally so that they make sense. It is important to remember that tactile symbols should be small enough to be felt by fingertips (approximately 1–2cm).

Large print users

Black and white maps are usually easier to access, as the detail is clearer with greater clarity and contrast. However, this does preclude colour clues. Unfortunately, coloured maps often lack contrast and symbol definition.

For some types of visual impairment, the most difficult task is to scan a map to locate symbols. This skill is needed for giving symbol coordinates, e.g. 'give the coordinates for an area of marshland'. Trying to find the marshland symbol within a multitude of colours, contour lines and coordinate lines is extremely difficult. Low-vision aids or video magnifiers should be encouraged where appropriate, but do not always make the task much easier. Finding symbols from given coordinates is a slightly easier task.

Braille users

The scanning difficulties described for print users also apply when scanning with fingertips. The only way to become adept at this is through continual practice. Pupils should learn to scan small areas at a time, working across the map in a methodical way. It is up to the teacher and pupil to decide how much importance should be attached to this skill in comparison with the number of times it will ever be used.

Review

OS work for pupils with visual impairment is time-consuming and tiring, and requires immense concentration. It is a difficult skill to acquire, requiring time and patience from both pupil and teacher.

8.4 Geography isn't just about maps!

The study of the environment, of peoples and places, trade and industry are central to geography and can all be accessible to pupils with visual impairment.

Textbooks

Geography textbooks often have a very busy layout that can be a visual nightmare for anyone with visual impairment. Layout often includes a variety of font styles and text is often superimposed over illustrations or patterned backgrounds. Enlarging on a photocopier is unlikely to be a satisfactory solution.

Encourage magnifiers and other low-vision aids whenever possible. Not only will this develop independence, but will also free up support hours for the modification of materials.

Videos and DVDs

When using videos or DVDs, consider the quality of the soundtrack. A soundtrack that relies heavily on visual images may be meaningless to pupils with little or no vision. Some DVDs do now include an audio description facility, which can be listened to through headphones. Relying on a live audio description in the classroom can be very distracting for other pupils and, unless the person doing it is experienced and has prepared a script in advance, may not be particularly effective.

Pupils with some useful vision may benefit from the opportunity to view in advance. This will allow viewing at close range without blocking the view of others. It is also possible to link the television to a laptop so that the video or DVD can be viewed simultaneously on the laptop screen.

Studying the local area

Here is an example of a non-visual approach to studying the local area.

- Obtaining information – In addition to maps and text resources, audio sources can provide information about facilities, public transport links, car parking and distances from other locations, etc. A telephone call to information lines, to local bus and train companies and taxi firms is a useful and realistic way of obtaining information. As evidence of the research, scripts can be prepared in advance and included in the final presentation.

- Visiting the location – Include pupils with visual impairment in visits. An additional member of support staff may be necessary to accompany pupils with visual impairment. Encourage other pupils to help describe features to pupils with visual impairment.

- Presenting information – It may be more difficult for pupils with severe visual impairment to include their own graphical material. Consider alternative formats for submitting information, e.g. audio recordings.

8.5 Globe work

Most commercial globes have no useful tactile information. To introduce pupils with visual impairment to globes, a specialist globe may need to be purchased or an existing globe adapted, as described below.

Specialist globes

Small Earth models made of foam are available from Learning Resources (www.learningresources.co.uk); they have raised land masses and mountains in relief, although the moulding is not sharply defined. These models are useful in the classroom as the model will fit in the hand and is useful for giving a tactile overview of the Earth. However, the material is difficult to label in braille and there is no axis.

Talking globes are available from Leap Frog (www.leapfrogshop.co.uk). These have limited use because the globes are not tactile. However, they are useful for learning facts, for listening skills and for making globe work more interesting.

Adapting standard globes

Some commercial globes have raised relief and can be useful for teaching about mountain ranges. Globes made with a raised or indented equator are extremely useful; pupils benefit from using the equator as a starting point. Likewise, a globe with obvious north and south poles is useful for establishing a starting point when exploring the globe. Globes that turn on an axis are preferable; they can be used to successfully teach about the movement of the Earth. Globes should be small enough for pupils to stretch their arms right around them; this gives a better spatial idea of locations.

Use textured shapes to mark continents, etc. It is not advisable to outline countries, as this can be very confusing. Land masses need to be thick enough to raise them up from the sea area. Materials should be flexible to follow the globe contours; the best option is sticky-backed plastic.

Wikki Stix are useful for marking places on a globe. They can be used to build mountain ranges, add rivers or plot journeys. Various sizes of self-adhesive Bumpons can be used to mark cities, volcanoes, etc. (Wikki Stix and Bumpons are available from RNIB).

Place names can be labelled with plastic braille labels or film. Large print labels are easily made on a computer.

A useful exercise is for pupils themselves to adapt a globe. This gives further opportunity for spatial awareness of places, and their proximity.

Using globes

Exploring globes is a difficult skill and requires support. Pupils with visual impairment benefit from working in pairs with sighted peers. They usually need help to track around the globe. Pupils usually need to be guided to feel north and south as they are used to mainly tracking horizontally rather than vertically. Pupils often enjoy keeping their finger in one position while the globe is spun beneath their hands. They can feel different areas moving past their fingers, and this helps them to understand the movement of the Earth, relationships between countries and distances. The more opportunities pupils have to freely explore a globe, the more they will recognise features.

To introduce the relationship between a two-dimensional map and a globe, roll a tactile or large print map of the world into a cylinder and hold the ends together with paper clips.

8.6 River studies

Rivers are a difficult concept for pupils with visual impairment because of their varying sizes and the differences in the landscapes that surround them. Practical experience of different types of river, e.g. crossing over bridges, jumping streams, crossing on a ferry, helps pupils gain a better understanding of the diversity of rivers.

Rivers can also be demonstrated successfully using three-dimensional models. Build models on a tray with raised sides so that any water used in a demonstration does not flow everywhere; this also enables the model to be moved around. Models are best made from air-hardening or fired material for demonstration, as mouldable putty and unfired clay become slimy when wet, which makes tactile exploration difficult.

Flow

Pupils with visual impairment often have problems understanding that water only flows downwards. Always check this basic knowledge, and if necessary do practical demonstrations using sloping troughs, pieces of guttering, etc. Pouring water down a slide works very well; pupils can also experience the sensation of 'down flow' themselves on a slide!

Meanders

Meander-type bends can be made with Wikki Stix, string or raised lines. Meandering rivers and ox bow lakes can be demonstrated by building models.

Banks

Use models to demonstrate high banks that keep the water in. The concept of a river flowing below the bank is spatially more difficult. A visit to a river bank, where stones can be dropped down into the water is the best experience, but if not possible then demonstrate using anything where the pupil can stand higher than the floor and look down at the river, e.g. chairs, stairs, boxes, etc.

Flooding and damming

Flooding and damming can be demonstrated with a model made of modelling clay (it takes a while to ensure it is watertight), or with a piece of guttering.

Erosion

Objects that demonstrate an abrasive action make a good introduction to erosion, e.g. sandpaper, grater. Use real pebbles and stones to examine types of rock: rub them together, roll them over sand, etc. Compare smooth and rough surfaces.

In a bowl or tank, pour water over a mixture of soil, sand, pebbles and stones (gravel for fish tanks works well), and feel what happens to the surface before and after: how is each size of particle affected? Use taps, jugs, etc. to demonstrate different forces of water.

Source to delta

A tried-and-tested method of modelling source to delta is using the pupil's own arm: place the palm flat on the table with fingers spread out and lift elbow up (most pupils need help to do this). Then using the other hand, follow the course of the river: shoulder is the source (highland), arm is the river flowing downwards, elbow is a river bend, hand is the river on a flat floodplain, fingers are distributaries formed when silt blocks the river flow on the flat land. Pupils find this demonstration easy to remember.

Water cycle demonstration kits from most educational catalogues are very useful; a model of the river landscape is very good for tactile exploration of flow, high–low land, lakes, etc. An adult can gently pour water onto the model and pupils can feel the water flow past their fingers (use coloured water for partially sighted pupils).

Resources

Water cycle kits are available from many education resource suppliers.

- Visit the River Ocean Foundation website for more resources (www.riverocean.org.uk).

CHAPTER 9

History

9.1 Teaching history

We live in a visual society and, for the majority of us, over 80 per cent of our learning is through vision. Many history resources and source materials are highly visual in nature, requiring pupils to sort through information presented in a variety of formats, e.g. photographs, textbooks, artefacts, maps and diagrams, etc. History teaches pupils important skills such as interpreting, evaluating and communicating information. These skills are vital to pupils with visual impairment who require strategies to evaluate the incomplete information they can access about the world around them. The whole class can benefit from using other senses in the exploration of history topics.

Sounds

- Turn off the picture on a video or DVD (or use an audio recording) of a historical battle and turn the volume up really loud so that the sound becomes overwhelming. Discuss the feelings that this produces.

- Use extracts from historical drama to provide an idea of the background sounds of a given period (e.g. horses on cobbled streets, street cries, even the lack of today's constant background noise).

- Study the different uses of language throughout history.

Smells

- Smells are not so easy to bring into the classroom, but fun to consider on a field trip to an outside location, such as a castle or reconstructed village.

- Discuss the types of smells that would pervade life then and now.

- Explore cooking methods and the types of food eaten.

Texture and touch

- Explore different types of fabrics that might have been used for clothing.

- On field trips and visits, consider the different surfaces, such as the hard cold walls of a castle, compared with the smooth wood panelling of a later dwelling.

- Given advance warning, many museums, etc. will arrange access for pupils with visual impairment to touch items that would otherwise be kept out of reach.

Role play

- Think about how people in given situations may have felt – empathise.
- Radio interviews develop good verbal description.
- Mock courtroom trials provide opportunities for questioning to concentrate on evidence gained through all the senses.

Using the ideas

- Write a diary of a given historical character, concentrating on all the senses.
- Use drama with plenty of sound effects, or create a soundscape.
- Visit local and national museums to try on historical costumes.
- Write a descriptive advertisement for an item of period clothing.
- Have a themed day (e.g. a Victorian day) when pupils dress in the clothes of the period and spend the school day as would a child of that time.
- Create an 'agony aunt' column with questions and answers relating to situations that could have arisen during the period being studied (e.g. a husband away at the Crusades, or a girl mistreated by her employer).

Conclusion

Once you start to explore multi-sensory ideas, one idea will lead to another and the whole experience will enrich both teaching and learning.

9.2 Using graphical sources

The history curriculum relies on many graphical sources; charts, tables, maps, photographs and cartoons. Some are included purely to provide information; others demand a degree of critical observation to draw conclusions. If you can establish the purpose of the source, the task of presenting the information in an accessible format becomes less daunting. The most appropriate solution can become apparent by asking the question 'What information is the pupil required to obtain from this source?'

Key action points

- A simple table can be rewritten as a list of statistics.
- In maps, avoid all unnecessary detail. Whether providing an enlarged or a tactile version, stick to a simple outline map with only the information needed. Building up information in a series of overlays may be less confusing than putting all the information onto a single sheet (see 8.2 Accessible maps).
- When using photographs, cartoons and other pictures, a good-quality original is vital if enlargement is to be of any value, whether using a magnifier or a photocopier. Verbal descriptions of pictures need to focus on the important features, and avoid vocabulary that relies on visual experience, particularly if working with pupils with no vision. Take care not to interpret the picture in the description.

- For tactile learners, it may be possible to produce a simple raised diagram that will provide the key information. Specialist equipment for producing more complex tactile diagrams is also available, ask the specialist teacher for guidance (see 4.4 Tactile diagrams).

Resources

- A specialist video magnifier system can be an invaluable aid to some pupils. Your local authority sensory support service should be able to advise and possibly provide access technology (see 4.10 Access technology).
- The Living Pictures Trust (www.livingpaintings.org) has produced a wide range of accessible pictures for pupils with visual impairment.

CHAPTER 10

Information and Communication Technology

10.1 Access to applications

Pupils access many learning materials by computer, much of it visual. Pupils with visual impairment use a range of access technology in their daily lives. Access technology includes screen readers, screen magnifiers, braille displays, braille notetakers and scanners. All of these can help pupils with visual impairment use computers effectively (see 4.10 Access technology).

Navigating with the keyboard

Many pupils with visual impairment find it difficult to use a mouse. Here are some strategies to navigate using the keyboard.

Keyboard shortcuts
Search the software help function using keywords such as 'accessibility' and 'keyboard shortcuts'. Print out a list of shortcuts and encourage pupils to use them; other pupils may also find these useful.

Common navigation keys

- Cursor keys for navigation left, right, up, down.
- Enter key for actions (mimicking the double click of a mouse).
- Space bar for marking check boxes or radio buttons (mimicking the single click of a mouse).
- Tab for moving from area to area, also Shift + Tab for the opposite direction.
- Page up, page down for scrolling up and down the screen.
- Function keys (i.e. F1, F2, F3, etc.) are specific to different software.
- Alt or Alt + F often opens up a set of drop-down menus; these menus can be explored using the cursor keys.
- Esc often allows exit from an area or menu.

Changing display settings

Many display settings can be changed to improve accessibility. Screen resolution, background colour schemes and text size and colour can all be changed using 'accessibility' and 'display settings' in the control panel. Most applications have a zoom setting to enlarge the view, but this does not alter menu text size; this must be done in 'display settings'. For networked computers, changes may need to be made by an ICT administrator, as many networks do not allow individual users to make these changes.

ICT vocabulary

Much of the vocabulary used in ICT is visual, with instructions about clicking on icons, dragging, highlighting text, etc. Pupils with visual impairment may need more precise language and additional help following instructions.

What to do if things don't work properly

- Use software help facilities (usually press F1) or search for help on manufacturers' websites.
- Contact software publishers and ask for help or even for a re-programmed version of the package.
- Contact screen reader producers, e.g. Supernova (www.yourdolphin.com) or Jaws (www.freedomscientific.com). Remember there may be newer versions available that may help solve your problems.
- Check that a screen reader has loaded the correct maps for that package.

Useful resources

- Contact software publishers and ask about accessibility.
- Search the internet using keywords such as 'computer accessibility', 'shortcut keys', 'keyboard shortcuts' and 'screen readers'.
- Visit Sarah Morley's home page of tutorials and advice on using Windows (www.winguide.co.uk).

10.2 Working with word processors

Using word processors is a hugely important skill in the modern world. Here are some strategies to help pupils with visual impairment access word processors. These strategies are for Microsoft Word; you should be able to adapt these strategies for most word processors.

Keyboard shortcuts and function keys

Keyboard shortcuts enable pupils to operate functions quickly using the keyboard without searching the menus. Table 10.1 below shows some common shortcuts.

Function keys also enable pupils to use the keyboard to access functions. Table 10.2 below gives some common function keys.

Keeping to a formula
It is important to always approach tasks the same way. For example, always use Ctrl + O to open a document, always use F12 to save and so on. It will soon become second nature.

Table 10.1

Ctrl + A	select all	Ctrl + M	indent a paragraph from left
Ctrl + B	bold	Ctrl + N	new document
Ctrl + C	copy	Ctrl + O	open an existing document
Ctrl + D	full font and effect changing	Ctrl + P	print
Ctrl + E	centre text	Ctrl + S	save
Ctrl + F	find	Ctrl + T	create a hanging indent
Ctrl + G	go to a particular place	Ctrl + U	underline
Ctrl + H	find and replace	Ctrl + V	paste
Ctrl + I	italic	Ctrl + W	close the current window
Ctrl + J	full justification	Ctrl + X	cut
Ctrl + K	insert a hyperlink	Ctrl + Y	redo
Ctrl + L	left justification	Ctrl + Z	undo

Table 10.2

F1	help
F7	spell check
F8	start a marked block
F12	save as
Home	jump to start of line
End	jump to end of line
Ctrl + Home	jump to start of document
Ctrl + End	jump to end of document

Using bookmarks

Bookmarks help pupils return to a particular place in a document, perhaps to put in a date that needs looking up, or a postcode that isn't remembered at the time. This can be particularly useful for examinations or homework where pupils might want to go back to a particular question. Here is a strategy for using bookmarks.

- At the place you wish to return to later, press Alt + I then K.
- Type in a reminder, e.g. date or postcode or q3.
- Press the Enter key.
- To find the reference again press Ctrl + G.
- Type in the reminder word and press the Enter key.
- The cursor moves to the place where the reminder was typed.
- Press Esc to get rid of the dialogue box.

Using the Microsoft Word spell checker with the keyboard

- Move the cursor to the start of the text (Ctrl + Home).
- Press F7.
- Read the word to the left of the cursor to check which word has been misspelled. Correct the spelling if you can and then press Alt + C to enforce the change.
- If you do not know the correct spelling, examine the alternatives by pressing Tab and using the up and down cursors.
- To ignore a spelling press Alt + I.
- To add a word to the dictionary press Alt + A.

10.3 Working with spreadsheets

Here are some strategies to help pupils with visual impairment access spreadsheets. These strategies are for Microsoft Excel; you should be able to adapt these strategies for most spreadsheets.

Editing a cell

As you move around the spreadsheet you have a view of the contents of the cells, but if you try to write in them once something is already written into the cell it will be overwritten. Each cell in a spreadsheet should be treated as a tiny word processor document. Press F2 to enter the cell to edit it; press Enter to exit the cell.

Finding your way around

To get to a particular cell press F5, type in the cell reference and press the Enter key. If you get lost, press Ctrl + Home to take you to cell A1.

Adjusting the width of a column

If too much is written in a cell for the width of the column, some of the contents will be hidden and a screen reader may not read it properly. Here is a method of preventing this.

- Move to the cell that contains the longest data entry in the column.
- Enter Excel's format menu by pressing Alt + O.
- Select the column option by pressing C.
- Select AutoFit Selection by pressing A.

Copying cells

- Move to the cell you want to copy and press F8.
- Press F5 and type the cell you want to copy to. Then press the Enter key. (This highlights the block.)
- Press Ctrl + D to copy down, or Ctrl + R to copy to the right.

Inserting a chart

Highlight the relevant cells with F8 and F5 as described above. Use Alt + I, followed by H to enter the chart wizard and follow the instructions. (For the default column chart just highlight the cells you want to use and press F11.)

Useful keys

All the usual commands used in Word also work in Excel, such as save, new, close, cut, copy, paste, bold, underline, etc. Here are some additional useful commands.

Table 10.3

F2	edit a cell and read a formula
F5	go to a specific cell
Ctrl + 1	cell format features
Ctrl + Z	undo last action
Ctrl + Y	redo what you just undid!

10.4 Working with databases

Here are some strategies to help pupils with visual impairment access databases. These strategies are for Microsoft Access; you should be able to adapt these strategies for most databases.

Reading a database table

Familiarise pupils with table layout. Each table is set out in the same way as a spreadsheet with columns and rows. Each cell is a field; each column contains all the references to one particular field for every record. Imagine a table containing details of names and addresses: if you go up or down the first column using the cursor keys you will read all the first names. Each row is a record; to read a whole record, move left to right using Tab or cursors.

Searching a table

To search the whole table it must first be highlighted. Move to any cell in the table. Press Ctrl + A (this highlights everything in the table). Press Ctrl + F, type in a word or phrase you are searching for and press Enter. Press Esc and examine the record. To find the next occurrence repeat the procedure.

Starting a new table

Press Alt + I then T. Use the down cursor key to find design view and press Enter. The design view is in three columns; field name, data type and description. You can move between these columns using the cursor keys; only the field name and data type are essential. In design view many cells contain drop-down lists. To activate a list in a cell press F4 and use the up and down keys to explore the options. To save your table press Ctrl + S. Close the design form by pressing Ctrl + W. To choose a field as a key field find the field in design mode. Press Alt + E followed by K. Save your table.

What to do if things don't work properly

Sometimes in databases, a screen reader loses focus because it does not know which of the open items it should be reading. Hold down the Alt key and tab through the open windows until you come to the one you want. Focus is then restored.

Useful keys

Table 10.4

F2	edit a cell
F6	move to the property pane in design view
Shift + Tab	tab backwards
Ctrl + W	close a window
Esc	use Esc instead of Enter when leaving a drop-down list so that you do not get lost

CHAPTER 11

Literacy

11.1 General issues

Communication and language provide a basis for all learning. People with visual impairment rely on effective use of language in a world that is becoming increasingly visual. From an early age, pupils with visual impairment should be encouraged to develop their communication and language skills to their full potential.

Incidental reading

Pupils with visual impairment often have reduced access to incidental reading. As sighted pupils learn to read and write, they are surrounded by print in advertisements, signs, leaflets, on the television, etc. These sources of reading are not equally available to pupils with visual impairment. As a result, pupils with visual impairment may find it more difficult to acquire the concept that language can be represented by print or braille symbols.

It might be necessary, for example, to check that a young person with visual impairment has had access to a newspaper before asking them to design a newspaper front page as a way of developing understanding of a reading book or novel.

Speaking and listening

Speaking and listening skills are particularly important to pupils with visual impairment, as the world is not full of accessible text. In some situations, it may be more appropriate for pupils with visual impairment to listen rather than read, or to speak rather than write. Encourage attention to detail, with correct use of grammar and syntax.

Additional time

Pupils with visual impairment often have difficulties with skimming, scanning and locating information on a page or in a book. Reading and writing are often slower tasks for pupils with visual impairment, and they may tire easily. Where possible, encourage pupils to take learning materials home and read them before they are used in the classroom. This will help pupils to engage in classroom activities rather than spend the whole lesson attempting to read material that their peers can read in a fraction of the time.

Short high-impact sessions in spelling or sentence construction and structuring can be too fast for pupils with visual impairment, who have to search more carefully for words, patterns, etc., or who may need to have visual information conveyed to them. They can easily become confused and get left behind, left out and consequently frustrated and demotivated. It is important to make space for occasional longer sessions, and sometimes to allow one-to-one time for pupils to complete the same tasks at their own pace.

Spelling

Pupils with severe visual impairment often have poor spelling skills. As spelling is largely a visual skill, this is not surprising. Use a structured spelling programme that does not rely on visual patterns and adopt a multi-sensory approach, producing letters with a textured surface from materials such as sandpaper and sticky-backed plastic. Three-dimensional letters can also be helpful. Braille spelling will require specialist input from a specialist teacher.

Classroom strategies

- Ensure pupils are positioned appropriately in the classroom – some pupils may need to sit at the front of the classroom whilst others may prefer to sit further back to get a clearer view.
- All pupils should have access to materials presented on the board. Pupils may be given print/braille copies, individual whiteboards or view information on a laptop connected to an interactive whiteboard.
- Create banks of braille and large print word cards that can be fitted together to form sentences, or to move clauses around within sentences.
- Increased concentration and memory demands may lead to increased fatigue and reduced motivation. Pupils may require additional support to keep them focused and motivated.

11.2 Learning to read and write print

Presenting materials

Initially, the large clear letter shapes used in infant classrooms are likely to suffice. However, as pupils progress through school, print sizes in resource materials and reading books are likely to get smaller and materials may need to be modified. Consider using individual magnifiers or a video magnifier, which magnifies the image onto a screen. Teachers should work closely with specialist teachers and support staff to ensure appropriate materials are provided.

Classroom strategies

- Avoid reading books that have text superimposed on illustrations or busy backgrounds.
- Three-dimensional letters that can be handled are sometimes helpful for learning letter shapes, e.g. magnetic letters. Tactile surfaces also add an extra dimension and can give a better sense of the shape of individual letters. Sandpaper, plastic foam, synthetic fur, velvet, polyester and suede all provide contrasting textures.

- Try drawing letter shapes in a sand tray, making the shapes from pipe cleaners, Wikki Stix or modelling dough.

- Teachers often use small arrows to indicate the direction in which a letter is formed. This may be too small or indistinct for pupils with visual impairment. Hand-over-hand modelling and practice is effective. An alternative is to use stencils with a brightly coloured dot to indicate the starting point.

- If standard lined writing paper is inappropriate, use paper with wider spaced and/or bolder lines.

- Pupils with visual impairment often have difficulty scanning whole words and sentences. Additional time may be needed to complete reading and writing tasks.

Resources

- The RNIB National Library (www.rnib.org.uk) provides giant-print library (size 24 point books) and offers a free postal service.

- The National Blind Children's Society's (www.nbcs.org.uk) CustomEye books is a large print book service, tailor-made to suit each child's eye condition.

- RNIB supplies thick-lined and raised-line paper (www.rnib.org.uk).

- Thick-lined and different colour line papers are available from stationery suppliers.

- Alternatively, you can produce customised paper on your computer. The accompanying resources CD contains a variety of different formats for lined papers.

- Wikki Stix are available from RNIB.

11.3 Learning to read and write braille

Specialist teachers for visual impairment are responsible for coordinating braille teaching. A specialist teacher and/or support staff will work closely with pupils to introduce braille as the rest of the class learn to read print. However, pupils with severe visual impairment should also be included in whole-class reading and writing activities as much as possible.

Pre-reading activities for young children

Like learning to read print, it is important to provide appropriate pre-reading activities to develop the necessary skills. Pre-reading activities can be modified to include tactile and other sensory experiences that may benefit all pupils in the classroom.

- Give pupils objects when reading stories to develop word association and help pupils with visual impairment feel included. Including pupils with visual impairment when reading stories helps pupils learn that reading is a social activity and that stories and ideas can be shared.

- Make story bags for books containing objects from the story.

- Make tactile books; this activity can include all pupils in the classroom. Use materials such as fur, aluminium foil, buttons, string, wool, etc.

- Encourage pupils to feel the tactile book whilst listening to a story and to turn the pages at the same time as the class teacher.

- Introduce activities to help pupils develop fine tactile differentiation. Placing different textured materials in a covered box for pupils to guess the material is a fun activity that the whole class can enjoy.

Learning braille

The braille alphabet is not usually taught in the same order as the print alphabet. Pupils initially learn to read letters and basic punctuation. Capital letters are not always used in braille; class teachers should check with those teaching braille if pupils are using capitals or not to avoid confusion in the classroom. Pupils may progress to grade 2 braille, as appropriate, which introduces short forms and contractions. Pupils learn to write braille using a Perkins brailler or a braille notetaker; these are usually provided by a sensory support service. For more information on braille, see 4.3 Braille.

Introducing basic braille to all pupils in the class can help pupils with visual impairment feel included. Ask your visiting specialist teacher to organise a braille awareness session with pupils and/or staff. Some schools organise braille clubs for pupils to learn to read and write basic braille. This helps encourage interaction between pupils with visual impairment and their peers.

Resources

- Revealweb (www.revealweb.org.uk) is a database of resources in modified formats, as well as an increasing number of electronic and digital versions.

- The RNIB National Library (www.rnib.org.uk) holds Europe's largest collection of braille and Moon books and provides a free postal library service.

- Braille versions of children's books are available from ClearVision (www.clearvisionproject.org). ClearVision books all have braille, print and pictures making them suitable for sharing. ClearVision also has tactile books available to loan.

- The National Blind Children's Society (www.nbcs.org.uk) produces braille books on request at the cost of the original.

- Bag Books (www.bagbooks.org) supply complete packs for telling stories with sensory additions.

11.4 Learning resource materials

Presenting materials

An assessment of functional vision by a specialist teacher will determine appropriate formats for reading and writing (see 5.3 Assessment of functional vision). For pupils who are able to access print, a range of presentation issues will need to be considered, including font size and type, paper size, use of coloured paper, text and illustrations, use of contrast, preferred type and colour of writing implements, use of sloping boards, etc. See Chapter 4 Materials and equipment for more information on presenting learning materials in print and braille.

As pupils progress through school, print sizes in resource materials and reading books are likely to get smaller and materials may need to be modified. Consider using individual magnifiers or a video magnifier, which magnifies the image onto a screen. Teachers should work closely with specialist teachers and support staff to ensure appropriate materials are provided.

Learning resource materials for pupils with visual impairment should be modified according to individuals' needs. Many learning resource materials, including text-books and assessment materials, incorporate visual layout and illustrations. When providing materials for use in the classroom or for assessment, these visual aspects must be considered.

Layout

Materials such as leaflets may be spread over a number of pages in large print and braille. This may influence pupils' responses when discussing layout and presentation. Avoid learning materials that have text superimposed on illustrations or busy backgrounds.

Illustrations

For some pupils with visual impairment, an enlarged copy of an illustration is the most appropriate form of conveying information; for others, a simplified version is more effective. For some pupils, however, verbal descriptions are required. When creating a description, it is important to find a balance between detail and length – too much additional reading is not always helpful. A description should concentrate on about three key points, and should remain objective, e.g. a shopper could be described as 'carrying five bags', rather than 'loaded down'.

11.5 Reading for pleasure

Many teachers can find it difficult to engage pupils in reading as a pleasurable and worthwhile leisure activity. For pupils with visual impairment, this change of per-ception can be even harder to achieve. A number of barriers can be identified, and, with some flexibility and imagination, solutions can be offered to make reading more accessible and enjoyable.

Access to reading materials

Finding books in an appropriate format is difficult. Research commissioned by RNIB shows that 96 per cent of books are not available in large print, audio or braille (RNIB 2004). Another access issue, in many ways equally significant, is that of subject matter and range of choice. Young people with visual impairment are in a minority, and many commercially available large print books are not aimed at children and young people. Non-fiction works, such as biographies, are also more difficult to find.

Fatigue and reading position

Many of us find our most enjoyable times with a book take place when we relax: curled up on the sofa, reading in bed, etc. Use of access technology, the need to hold a book very close to the face or the bulkiness of braille and large print can all make it difficult to associate reading with relaxation. Postures can be difficult to maintain for a long time, and some eye conditions lead to fatigue very quickly. It is important that those who work with pupils are aware that while access technology makes print more accessible, it does not solve everything, and can bring fatigues of its own.

Censorship of reading material

Pupils with visual impairment often have a much narrower experience of what is available to them; sighted people may dictate their choices, as browsing through titles may not always be easy. It is important that pupils are given access to a wide range of titles and authors.

Solutions

How can we overcome or find ways around these barriers? Simply being aware that they exist can help to plan work with pupils in a different way: being aware of fatigue can ensure that we allow an activity to cease or have breaks before it becomes onerous; we can create opportunities for stretching, or moving around. Enabling pupils to manage their own fatigue in this way can lead them towards becoming aware of and taking control of their own work patterns.

Electronic formats can be created with a scanner, which pupils can then interact with independently – either by printing a copy or using screen magnifiers or screen readers on a computer.

Finally, the spoken word can be a very powerful way of widening pupils' experiences of both fiction and non-fiction. Although this will not be an aid to improving the technical aspects of pupils' reading and writing, it can work significantly to develop an appreciation for reading. Reading aloud is perhaps the most powerful way of sharing one's own love and enjoyment of a book.

Resources

See 18.3 Obtaining accessible learning resource materials for sources of accessible format reading books.

11.6 Coursework

In many ways, coursework for external qualifications can be a valuable opportunity for pupils with visual impairment to demonstrate their ability and understanding without the added time pressure of examinations. Coursework offers the time and space to re-draft and check over their work, with opportunities to ensure that spelling and presentation reflect understanding and ideas. However, there are some areas, such as those described below, where pupils may need extra support.

References and quotations

Skimming and scanning through texts can present problems, as bulky braille and large print can be very off-putting and time-consuming. Ensure that pupils have support with this, as close reference to texts is often a requirement of coursework.

Support staff need to be aware that pupils may not be quoting directly because they are daunted by the mass of text they will have to plough through, word by word, if they are unable to scan easily. Encourage pupils to identify the section of the text, or the event they wish to refer to, and then to narrow down where in the book this appears. If necessary, support staff can then find the precise quote, and help pupils to compile a list of these as part of their planning process.

Checking work

Pupils may need additional time to re-draft and identify mistakes and to correct them. Again, they might not be able to gain an overview of the whole piece of work, so issues such as paragraphing, subheadings, layout, etc. may not be easily identified. Spelling errors, too, can be difficult to identify, especially if pupils are relying on screen readers for word processing. It can be very helpful at this stage to encourage pupils to print or emboss their work and to read the hard copy; this frequently makes pupils much more aware of repeated errors they had overlooked.

Fatigue

Fatigue can also be an issue. Pupils with visual impairment may need to take frequent breaks from extended writing tasks. Provide opportunities for them to take breaks without disrupting other pupils. Some disruptive behaviour in the classroom may sometimes be a pupil's method of taking a break from the fatigue of writing or staring at a screen.

Learning concepts

There may be times when a pupil's understanding of concepts might need to be verified; gaps in blind pupils' perceptions of the world are a well-documented phenomenon (see Warren 1994, Chapter 3) and it is important to verify that these do not have an impact on pupils' understanding of texts, themes and ideas. For example, when teaching *Romeo and Juliet*, a teacher may progress well into the text before realising that a number of pupils are unsure about what a balcony is. Talking – and listening carefully – to pupils is often the best way to pick up issues like this, and a curriculum area such as literacy can be very fruitful for broadening pupils' understanding and experiences through the very nature of the subject matter and the wide opportunity for discussion.

11.7 Revision techniques

Revision can be particularly difficult for pupils with visual impairment as techniques for skimming and scanning which pupils are encouraged to develop are not always possible. Here are some effective revision techniques that may work for all pupils equally well.

Planning answers

One area of literature and reading that can be challenging is finding and using examples and quotations. The amount of time used by pupils to find these under examination conditions can outweigh any additional time allowance quite considerably.

Encourage pupils to spend time planning answers and finding quotations for sample questions without necessarily going on to write the essay. This helps form a picture of where incidents occur within a text and the way that themes cross through texts, and provides opportunities to identify and find appropriate quotations without examination time restrictions.

Revision tapes

Pupils with visual impairment often find it easier to learn material from audio recordings. This reduces fatigue from the physical demands of reading, enabling pupils to concentrate on the content of the material. Audio recordings can take the form of taped notes, summarising plot lines, describing characters, themes, etc., or they can be used to provide quotes in an easily memorable form. Recordings can be created by the pupils themselves, providing revision and reinforcement opportunities as well as collaborative tasks. Once created, copies can be made for the entire group.

Quizzes, mini tests and short-answer revision exercises

Quizzes, mini tests and short-answer revision exercises often work best electronically – pupils can record their answers electronically, which cuts down on unwieldy difficult-to-find answer boxes, or having to write out answers on separate pages.

11.8 Braille and bilingual pupils

Background

Bilingualism is the ability to use two different languages. Historically, pupils with visual impairment were taught monolingually with braille taught only in the majority language. However, in today's society many people are bilingual and schools are likely to include pupils from a range of linguistic backgrounds, for whom English may not be their most proficient language. Pupils with visual impairment may have existing braille skills in a language other than English. In bilingual countries, such as Wales, provision must be made for learning through both languages for all pupils.

Challenges

It may be difficult to find a proficient professional with the ability to teach braille in a language that is not their own first language, e.g. a non-Welsh-speaking professional endeavouring to teach Welsh braille to pupils in a bilingual education setting. Braille courses in languages other than English are available, e.g. the Welsh braille course.

Another challenge for teachers involved in supporting bilingual learning for pupils with visual impairment is the lack of visual incidental learning of the second language. Although it is possible to acquire a language verbally, visual incidental learning is restricted. Additional time and resources may be needed to help pupils acquire an additional language.

Moving on

Strategies for introducing additional languages include creating 'text rich' environments, e.g. labelling of toys, cupboards, trays, drawers and resources. Pupils learning braille often benefit if their own families learn braille in the home language, with support from a sensory support service.

Social interaction and language development

Social interaction is crucial to the development of language skills. It is widely accepted that learning and development usually take place within social contexts. Pupils with visual impairment often depend on adults or peers to interpret events and to provide verbal descriptions, which can be a demanding task. Careful use of supporting adults and peers as mediators in social interactions is essential for the development of language in pupils with severe visual impairment.

Conclusion

Language is not only the means of expressing ideas but is also the basis for individuals to think and learn. Pupils with visual impairment can successfully acquire additional languages and associated braille skills. However, strategies must be put in place to ensure that incidental learning of the language is encouraged, using adults or peers as facilitators.

CHAPTER 12

Mathematics

12.1 General teaching strategies

Positioning

Pupils with visual impairment are likely to need to be close to the teacher or other focus of attention, even for oral work. Sometimes it may also be necessary to demonstrate a process on a one-to-one basis.

Additional time

Pupils with visual impairment need more time to complete tasks. Either give pupils additional time to perform tasks or modify tasks so that less work is needed.

Number skills

Pupils with visual impairment often miss out on early number experiences in everyday life. Sighted pupils are introduced to numbers in reading books and on television programmes from an early age. Do not presume that pupils with visual impairment have encountered these early experiences.

Pupils with visual impairment often find it difficult to grasp the concepts of whole numbers and zero. They will not view five people together in a room at a glance, or see that there are four chairs around a table. Pupils may not see patterns such as multiples of 10 in a 100-grid. Pupils of all ages may need time to practise counting, matching, ordering and comparing skills.

Estimation skills

Sighted pupils often use visual references to make estimates. Pupils with visual impairment may find estimation techniques difficult. Use real objects to teach measurement.

Practical tasks

Ensure that pupils have appropriate equipment, e.g. large print calculators, talking calculators, magnifiers, etc. Working with a partner is useful when fine measurements are needed; the sighted pupil can make the readings and the pupil with visual impairment can record the results.

Tactile materials

Pupils will need plenty of opportunities to handle actual objects and to experience the practical application of number, especially if they cannot see clearly their representation by two-dimensional means. Enhance learning number shapes with tactile materials and three-dimensional numbers.

Three-dimensional diagrams

Where possible, pupils with visual impairment should not be presented with three-dimensional diagrams. Use two-dimensional diagrams or give pupils the solid shapes.

Incidental learning

Displays, pictures and posters relating to number may be inaccessible to pupils with visual impairment. Provide individual copies, in appropriate formats (see 4.8 Visual displays).

12.2 Materials

Drawing, diagrams and grids

- Tactile diagrams may be presented on heat swell paper, drawing film, thermoform plastic or embossed on braille paper (see 4.4 Tactile diagrams). All of these media feel different and have different properties, e.g. the end of a line may not be as well defined on heat swell paper as on the others. Pupils will need experience of all media.

- Heat swell paper is generally used where diagrams do not require a response marked on the diagram, e.g. shape and space diagrams, or for simple diagrams that do not require different textures. A square grid on heat swell paper is extremely useful for work on a graph board, e.g. coordinates work.

- Drawing film is placed on a floppy (or jelly) mat for tactile drawing. One side of film adheres to the mat better than the other to keep the film in place. Tactile marks are made on the film with a stylus or a ballpoint pen with no ink, although it is sometimes useful (especially for the teacher) to use an ordinary ballpoint pen that will also leave a visual mark. Floppy mats can also be put onto a graph board for pins and bands to be used in addition to drawing. Film can be placed directly onto a graph board if only pins and bands are to be used.

  To add labels to a diagram on drawing film, first attach the film to a piece of braille paper using staples. This sheet can then be used in a Perkins or other brailler to add text. The braille paper makes the diagram more durable for storing in a pupil's file.

- Thermoform plastic can be placed on a graph board to use with pins and elastic bands for drawing and measuring, and for work using square grids and pie charts. Shape and space diagrams can also be created as a collage on braille paper and reproduced on thermoform plastic or drawing film using a thermoform machine.

- Use braille paper for simple statistical tables and charts, particularly early stage bar charts and for drawing pictograms using braille signs. Stem and leaf diagrams are usually produced on braille paper. Tiger embossers produce simple diagrams using raised dots on standard braille paper, and enable text and diagrams to be embossed on the same page.

Grids for print users

- A selection of graph papers and pie chart grids are available on the accompanying CD.

- RNIB produces a range of coloured graph paper and pie charts which are available to purchase.

- Create and print bespoke grids and graph papers using an online graph generator. The Incompetech PDF graph/grid generator is free to download from www.incompetech.com

Once you have found a size and colour of grid that a pupil finds accessible, this can be used for all graph work.

Resources

Floppy mats, drawing film, thermoform plastic, braille paper and a range of tactile and print graph papers, including embossed spur wheel grids, are available to purchase from RNIB and other suppliers listed in 18.1 Directory of suppliers.

12.3 Equipment

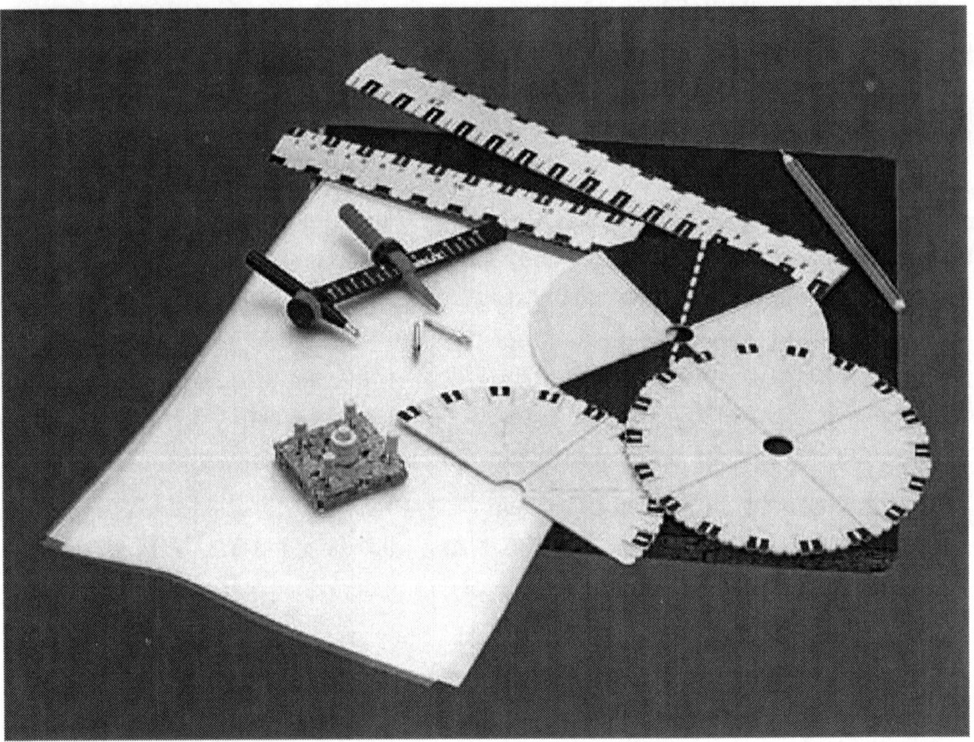

Figure 12.1 Tactile geometry set © RNIB

Tactile and other rulers

Tactile rulers are available in 20cm and 30cm lengths from RNIB; they are yellow with black markings to provide maximum contrast and are also useful for print users. Clear rulers with black markings are also available. The rulers are graduated in half centimetres, as pupils with visual impairment should be required to measure or draw to accuracy of 5mm only. One edge of the ruler has indentations, which may be put against pins for measuring. Some pupils may be able to use a well-marked standard ruler ignoring millimetre markings, if necessary.

Accessible angle measurers and protractors

RNIB supplies 360° and 180° angle measurers in yellow or clear, with black markings at 10° intervals with 5° subdivisions. Pupils with visual impairment should be required to measure angles to the nearest 5° only. RNIB also supplies a 360° angle measurer with 45° intervals. Some pupils may be able to use a well-marked standard 360° angle measurer ignoring the 1° graduations if necessary, or custom-made angle measurers can be produced on an acetate sheet using a photocopier. To use a tactile angle measurer, all lines should be at least 8cm long as the radius of the tactile angle measurer is 7.5cm.

 Angle measurer templates are available on the accompanying CD.

Compasses

Many pupils with visual impairment find standard compasses difficult to use and may prefer a bar compass or a ruler-style compass (available from RNIB as part of a geometry set). A ruler-style compass can take a stylus or felt-tip pen, which does not pull the paper as much as a ballpoint pen. If a standard compass is used, a supporting adult may need to open the compass to the specified size.

Graph boards

RNIB supplies a graph board (described as a geometry base); alternatively try making your own. Use unsealed cork tiles (approximately 30cm square) and glue together to make a board about 2cm thick, or cut up noticeboard material to the same size. It is important that pins can easily be pushed into the board, but if the board is too soft they do not stay in position. The board can be bound around the edges with strong tape, to ensure that the glued cork tiles do not come apart. This will make the board more pleasant to use and also prolong its life. Diagrams should be attached to the board with drawing pins, which are flat and don't get confused with the pins being used for plotting. Pins are used to identify points and elastic bands may be used for lines. Chart pins are available from RNIB, but any pins with a reasonably large head (to accommodate and retain the bands) and a sufficiently long shank (about 1cm) may be used. Mapping pins with larger hexagonal or round heads are useful for identifying special points, e.g. the origin of coordinates.

Floppy mats

Floppy mats (or jelly mats) are used with drawing film and are available from RNIB and other suppliers. They can also be mounted on a graph board if using pins as well as a stylus. When they lose their tackiness, this can be restored by hand washing in washing-up liquid.

Resources and other equipment

There is a range of other useful equipment available from RNIB and other suppliers – a browse in the RNIB online shop and the suppliers listed in 18.1 Directory of suppliers will reveal talking calculators, folding geometry shapes, clocks, specially designed mathematics activity kits and much more.

12.4 Drawing and measuring

Below are some suggestions for using the materials and equipment described in 12.2 and 12.3.

Measuring the length of a line with a tactile ruler

Put pins at each end of the line and then align the ruler with the pins. The indentations on one side of the tactile ruler may be put against the pins or the other side of the ruler may be used. Pupils should not be expected to measure a line with greater accuracy than ± 5mm.

Drawing a tactile line on drawing film

Use a tactile ruler to draw a line that is longer than required. Put a pin or mark at one end of the line and use a ruler to measure the length required, then put a pin on the line to mark it. Pins can be removed and the line marked where the pins have been. Keeping the ruler steady and drawing the line is difficult; if the ruler does not have non-slip gripping pads it may help to use adhesive putty (such as Blu-tack) to keep the ruler in place. Pupils should not be expected to a draw a line with greater accuracy than ± 5mm.

Measuring an angle with a tactile angle measurer

Use a tactile angle measurer (or protractor) that comes with a set of pins and a collar. The RNIB tactile angle measurer has a radius of 7.5cm; so all lines should be longer than this. Put a pin at the point of the angle, put the collar over the pin and the angle measurer over the collar. Secure the zero line on the angle measurer against one of the angle lines using a pin (best put in at an angle). Read the size of the angle by counting the markings on the angle measurer. Pupils should be expected to give angle measurements to the nearest 5° only.

Drawing an angle

Draw the baseline of the angle and put a pin in the line at the point where the angle is to be drawn. Put the collar and then the angle measurer over the pin. Secure the angle measurer with the pin ensuring that the zero line is against the base line. Read off the required angle and put a pin against the mark on the angle measurer. Remove the securing pin, then the collar and finally the angle measurer. Draw a line between the pin at the point of the angle and the one at the required angle and make the line the required length using a ruler as explained above.

Drawing arcs or complete circles

Choose compasses that take a stylus or ballpoint pen to draw arcs or complete circles. Unless the compasses have tactile markings, a supporting adult will need to adjust the radius as requested by the pupil. Fix the centre of the circle, either with the point of bar compasses or with a pin at the end of ruler compasses. Pressure has to be firm so that the line can be felt but the drawing film needs to stay in place; a lot of practice may be needed.

12.5 Charts, graphs and pictograms

Statistical charts

To modify a statistical chart, ensure the grid is large enough to enable drawing and labelling, e.g. 2cm grid for bar charts and frequency diagrams and very simple symbols for pictograms.

Labelling charts is very difficult for braille users. Pupils could place the chart in a Perkins brailler, or instruct a supporting adult to mark the scales. Supporting adults may need to ensure that pupils count up the intervals.

Bar charts for braille users

To introduce bar charts, use a brailler (Perkins or electronic) and the ⠿ ('for') sign to produce horizontal bars, e.g. six signs would represent a bar six units long. The completed chart will consist of bars of different lengths all starting at the same vertical axis. Work on bar charts can then progress to pins in squares on a graph board or marked squares on a film grid. Eventually a vertical bar chart can be made either by drawing outlines on drawing film or using pins and bands on a square grid on a graph board.

Pie charts for braille users

Pupils should construct their own pie charts on ready-made pie chart grids. Grids should be of at least 8cm radius marked in 10° sections with a cross or a large raised point or blob at the centre; some pupils find it easier if the markings extend beyond the circumference of the grid. Pupils can often estimate the necessary angle with sufficient accuracy and do not always need to use an angle measurer.

Completed pie charts for pupils to interpret may be prepared on heat swell paper with braille labels.

 Sample pie chart grids are available on the accompanying CD.

Pictograms for braille users

It is very difficult for braille users to reproduce pictogram symbols. Some braille symbols can be used, e.g. the ⠿ ('for') sign can be divided into either two parts vertically (⁚) or three parts horizontally (··). If a pictogram is to be read only, use very simple symbols, e.g. circles, rectangles or triangles, on heat swell paper.

Line graphs for braille users

If a permanent record is not needed, use a square grid on heat swell paper on a graph board. Plot coordinates using pins; use a large pin for the origin. Use a scale of one square to one unit if possible. Lines can be drawn using elastic bands. If a permanent record is needed, use a square grid on drawing film.

Graphs of curves

It is generally accepted that pupils with visual impairment are not able to interpret or draw graphs with the accuracy expected of their sighted peers.

To draw a curve, braille users can use Wikki Stix, pipe cleaners or Flexi Curves (made of a PVC outer casing, with a core of lead). If a permanent record is needed it is best for a supporting adult to transcribe the curve onto drawing film. Where axes are not labelled, if a pupil wishes to read values from a graph they have drawn, find a horizontal value by counting back to the vertical axis from the given point and vice versa.

Wikki Stix are available from RNIB. Flexi Curves are available from arts and crafts suppliers.

Other data presentation methods

Braille users may draw frequency polygons, cumulative frequency diagrams, histograms, box plots, etc. either with a stylus on plastic film or using pins and elastic bands on drawing film, thermoform plastic or heat swell paper. Use Wikki Stix, pipe cleaners or Flexi Curves to draw cumulative frequency curves.

Data may have to be modified substantially because of the restrictions imposed by using open square grids; e.g. decimal values cannot be plotted accurately. Pupils using print should be able to access these topics provided a suitable enlarged grid is used and the data is modified to give suitable values for the grid used.

12.6 Transformations

For pupils with moderate to severe visual impairment, use a coordinate grid to teach transformations. Use simple shapes without complicated diagonal lines and an open square grid (1cm, 1.5cm or 2cm). Braille users can use a square grid on a graph board with pins and elastic bands for classroom purposes. Permanent records can be made on drawing film.

Print users may find it useful to begin with a tactile grid, pins and elastic bands, as for braille users. Provide cut-out shapes for all pupils with visual impairment, where possible.

Translations

Teach the rule:

- all points move the same distance.

Plot the original shape on a grid with pins and elastic bands. Then, teach pupils to use the grid to count the required number of squares horizontally and vertically. Use co-ordinates to translate each point of the shape with pins. Finally use an elastic band to outline the translated shape.

Reflections

Teach the two rules:

- all movement is perpendicular to the mirror line
- the distance from the object point to the mirror line is equal to the distance from the mirror line to the reflection point.

Plot the original shape on a grid with pins and elastic bands. Then, use an elastic band or Wikki Stix to put in the mirror line. Plot the reflection using the method described above for translations. The mirror line can be seen as a line of symmetry for the completed diagram, so this method is a good way of teaching line symmetry.

Enlargement

Teach the two rules:

- the centre of enlargement, a point on the original shape and the corresponding point on the enlargement are in a straight line
- for an enlargement with scale factor k, the distance from the centre of enlargement to the point on the enlargement is k multiplied by the distance from the centre of enlargement to the corresponding point on the original shape.

Plot the original shape on a grid with pins and elastic bands. Then, use a pin to plot the centre of enlargement. To plot each point of the enlargement, count the squares from the centre of enlargement to the original shape and then multiply this number by the scale factor k. Count this number of squares in a straight line from the centre of enlargement and plot the point with a pin. Finally, use elastic bands to outline the enlargement.

To reinforce the first rule, use elastic bands to join the centre of enlargement to each point of the original shape and the corresponding point on the enlargement.

Rotation

Teach the rules:

- the distance between the centre of rotation and each point on the shape is unchanged by rotation
- the lines joining the centre of rotation to each point on the shape will rotate through the same angle
- for angles of rotation of 90°, horizontal lines in the original shape become vertical lines in the rotation and vice versa
- for angles of rotation of 180°, horizontal lines remain horizontal and vertical lines remain vertical.

Sighted pupils often use tracing paper for rotations and can rotate the shape by rotating the tracing paper. Pupils with visual impairment can use a graph board in the same way as a piece of tracing paper. First, plot the original shape on a grid with pins and elastic bands. Then, use a pin to plot the centre of rotation. Rotate each point separately through the required angle about the centre of rotation. This is best explained by using the two examples below:

Rotate a shape through 90° clockwise:

- note the coordinates of the original shape using the centre of rotation as the origin
- turn the graph board through 90° anti-clockwise
- re-plot the original shape with the board in this position
- turn the board back through 90° clockwise to its original position.

Rotate a shape through 180°:

- note the coordinates of the original shape using the centre of rotation as the origin
- turn the graph board through 180° (either way)
- re-plot the original shape with the board in this position using the coordinates
- turn the board back to its original position.

CHAPTER 13

Modern foreign languages

13.1 Teaching strategies

Pupils with visual impairment rely on oral communication to a greater degree than their sighted peers. Here are some suggestions to make teaching methods accessible to all pupils, particularly those with visual impairment.

Flash cards

Pupils should have individual copies of flash cards in an appropriate format. If this is not possible, a support assistant or a friend could whisper (in English) what is on the card. Consider using objects instead of, or to supplement, flash cards so that pupils with visual impairment can feel the objects; this clearly works better with topics such as fruit or clothes than topics such as weather.

Voice and use of language

Pupils with visual impairment should be taught visual language. Pupils need to understand commonly used language such as colours, e.g. that *verde* is the Spanish for 'green'. Continue to use instructions that contain 'seeing' words and phrases such as 'Look at page 23, can you see where the restaurant is?'

Movement

Mime is often used when teaching modern foreign languages. Where pupils have some useful vision, movements could be exaggerated. For pupils with severe visual impairment, supplement mime with oral description.

Presenting materials on the board

When presenting materials on a whiteboard, read out what you are writing; sighted pupils may also benefit from this.

Audio recordings

Presenting and recording material in audio format is helpful for pupils with visual impairment. Remember, if pupils are answering questions whilst listening to a recording, you will need to stop the recording to allow time for pupils to record their answers. Make sure a braille user has completed brailling before continuing so that noisy clattering keys do not obscure the next piece of dialogue. Pupils may also use a support assistant for recording answers.

Pairing

Encourage pupils with visual impairment to work in pairs with sighted peers, taking it in turns to answer questions.

Overhead projectors and interactive whiteboards

Pre-prepared transparencies can be photocopied and given to pupils for use in the lesson. Work presented on a whiteboard can be printed out in advance or in the lesson.

Games

Many pupils with visual impairment have well developed memory skills and team games can take advantage of this, using the sight of one pupil and the oral and listening skills of a pupil with visual impairment to report back.

Tasks

It will take pupils with visual impairment longer to complete tasks, so you can ask them to produce less than sighted pupils in the same time. Modify the task so that visually impaired pupils cover all they need to learn but less writing is required.

Planning and liaison

When planning lessons, ensure that you liaise with the support assistants to advise them of any resources you intend to use. Remember that adapting resources is very time-consuming and whoever does it will not appreciate being asked to prepare more material than will actually be used! Try not to change lesson plans at the last minute.

13.2 Adapting textbooks

Modern foreign language textbooks are often very visual with busy layouts. Features include maps, symbols, cartoons, fragmented page layouts, variable and small prints, cursive script, print in different colours and on different coloured backgrounds, punctuation and accents and photographs.

Adapting resources is time-consuming, especially when they need major modification rather than just straight enlargement. So, here are a few tips.

- Teachers and support staff should work together to decide if pupils need all of the information, or if some of it can be left out.

- If there are pictures for pupils to identify in the foreign language, such as shops, use words in place of the pictures – greengrocer, butcher, etc. This approach is common in modified external examination papers.

- Handwritten letters or materials in cursive script can be typed out in enlarged print or produced in braille.

- Go over accents in felt-tipped pen, as these are often difficult to see.

- Where possible, simplify exercises, e.g. when there is a series of advertisements for shops with telephone numbers and the exercise is asking what time the shop is open or what it sells, the telephone numbers are not required. Retrieval of information for pupils with visual impairment is much more time-consuming, so the exercise will still be a challenge, even with some of the non-essential information removed.

- Maps can be modified to include only material essential to the task, e.g. remove some of the non-essential roads and landmarks.

- For comprehension exercises, place questions before text so that pupils with visual impairment read the passage knowing what to look for. If the text is long you can split it in half with the questions for the first section before the first half and the questions for the second section before the second half. This is how external modern foreign language examination papers are usually modified.

- Finally, when adapting resources, keep in mind the desired outcome. It is not always necessary to reproduce materials so that they are exactly the same in modified large print or braille. Alternative presentation methods, e.g. aural presentation or recordings, may be more appropriate. Ask yourself what information pupils are expected to interpret, and how they can be given this information.

 See 4.5 Modifying learning resource materials and the accompanying CD for more suggestions and examples of modified learning resource materials.

13.3 Useful resources

Teachers

The best resource a pupil can have is a good teacher – never under-estimate yourself! The teacher can be the key to making a French, German or Spanish lesson come alive for pupils with visual impairment more than any book, tape or CD; this applies to support teachers and assistants too!

Braille code

Specialist braille codes are available from RNIB for French, Spanish and German.

Dictionaries

- French, German and Spanish large print dictionaries are available from RNIB (www.rnib.org.uk).

- Online dictionaries are useful; use with screen magnifiers or screen readers where necessary.

- Contact dictionary and textbook publishers and ask for electronic copies to use with screen readers, or to produce in large print or braille.

CHAPTER 14

Music

Pupils with visual impairment should be encouraged to take part in music. Listening to and making music helps develop aural skills, which are particularly important for pupils with visual impairment.

14.1 Reading and writing music

Here are some suggestions for making written music accessible for pupils with visual impairment.

- Check that pupils understand that sound can be represented by symbols.
- Begin with tactile symbols – place pasta, string or buttons on a tile with sticky putty to represent notes.
- Progress to scores on drawing film and swell paper, with a prepared horizontal line in the middle for orientation as a time-line or a particular pitch. Use a thin line joining 'events' for ease of tracking.
- Use pupils' hands to represent the music stave and spell out tunes on the fingers: for the treble clef label the little finger as E, the space between it and the ring finger F, the ring finger G, etc.
- Introduce enlarged or tactile note shapes for crotchets, minims, quavers (in various groupings), etc. to show how note tails go up and down.
- Present written music from the whiteboard in large print on individual mini whiteboards.
- Enlarge sheet music and tag into a book with a firm back and attractive cover or introduce braille music on clear pages in between the print. Stress to pupils with visual impairment that most of the group are mainly playing instruments by ear and just beginning to understand the notation. In practice times, encourage pupils to tap the rhythm and to sing the tune whilst reading and then memorise each piece.
- Modify complex sheet music and worksheets to remove all elements that are not going to be used. For some pupils, photocopy enlargement may be sufficient. However, the more a piece of music is enlarged, the less can be seen of it at any one time. Use computer software (e.g. Sibelius) to produce modified stave notation, which uses differential enlargement for different symbols, e.g. a staccato dot may need enlarging significantly whereas a treble clef may not need

enlarging at all. Notes may be enlarged while retaining the length of note tails and grouping to help with tracking.

- Encourage pupils to produce their own music notation using music technology: record on a music keyboard, check the piece by listening and then save and print out the stave notation.

Braille music

Music notation can be produced in braille using the braille music code. The specialist teacher for visual impairment can advise on teaching braille music. The braille music code is suitable for pupils who have an interest in music and are proficient braillists. It is rarely possible to read braille notation and play an instrument at the same time, so pupils should be encouraged to memorise music.

Resources

- Auto Press Education (www.autopresseducation.co.uk) produces mini white-boards A4-size with two large print staves on one side.
- The braille music code and resources are available from RNIB (www.rnib.org.uk) or from the Braille through Remote Learning website (www.brl.org/music).
- *Focus on Braille Music* by Lisette Wesseling (2004) is available in print and braille for pupils to use to learn braille music with adult encouragement.
- Transcription packages are available for braille music transcription. If there are sighted staff available with a basic knowledge of stave notation, Toccata is probably the easiest to use currently available (http://members.optusnet.com.au/~terryk/toccata.htm).
- Produce modified stave notation using mainstream notation packages such as Sibelius (www.sibelius.com), which is widely used in schools in the UK. This package has a huge range of options for altering symbol size and placing. Set up a 'preferred format' for each pupil after experimentation and import new files into this.
- Published large print and braille music is available from Revealweb (www.revealweb.org.uk) and the RNIB National Library (www.rnib.org.uk).
-  Examples of large print music notation staves are included on the accompanying CD.

14.2 Group music making

Pupils with visual impairment should be included in group music as much as possible. Group music provides valuable experiences for pupils to express themselves and develop team working skills. Here are some strategies for including pupils with visual impairment in group music.

- Position pupils close to the teacher where possible. If a pupil is not able to follow hand directions, a supporting adult or pupil could tap instructions and rhythms on the pupil's arm. Discuss this with the pupil in advance to find a method that they are comfortable with.

- Discuss the way pupils are going to start and end playing, particularly if they are to start or end all at the same time. One pupil could breathe in dramatically or use a hand gesture if accessible, or counting could be used.

- Encourage musical cues within the piece, such as pupil one starting a rhythm pattern and pupil two starting after four patterns.

- Discuss the shape of musical pieces noting points of silence or sudden changes in mood, which often means dynamic (volume) change.

- Rehearse separate parts so that all pupils are clear who does what. It is very easy to pick out just the main part (usually the top part) wherever it occurs, rather than when the melody line is mixed with accompaniment.

- If actions are being used in a choir song, have the group working in pairs holding hands 'mirror' acting. Pupils can take turns as leader, so pupils with visual impairment can learn the action and also the size and timing of the gesture.

- If using written materials, ensure the leader of the group is aware of alternative formats, particularly where page numbers and other layout does not match the main copy.

- For printed materials, consider formatting enlarged sheets into A4 landscape and placing in a hardback folder. A solid music stand, perhaps with a battery-operated light, may help. Use highlighter pens to mark individual parts, or for guiding from line to line in the music.

- Sighted musicians often read and perform at the same time. However, pupils with visual impairment are often unable to read whilst performing and need to play from memory. Try to ensure all teachers and support staff are aware of how far in advance music is required for memorisation.

- Audio recordings can help pupils learn lyrics and melody and get a feel for the accompaniment. Taping a rehearsal is sufficient for this where a pupil has a clear melodic part; other pieces may require a bespoke tape with fingering and other performance details spoken. For instrumental pieces, try to split pieces into phrases and leave silences of equal length so that pupils can repeat back without having to stop the tape.

- Memorising more complex pieces using audio recordings is hard work, especially if pupils need to keep picking up and putting down an instrument as well as operating the pause, play and rewind buttons. Singing the melody may speed up the memorisation. Software with sound and notation may be easier to navigate if the piece can be recorded into electronic format, e.g. MIDI.

Resources

- Use a good-quality pupil-operable portable recording device, such as a minidisc or MP3 player, along with high-fidelity playback equipment with headphones.

- Use solid but lightweight music stands with flexible height.

- Use a portable light to clip onto music sheets.

- Have a list of instruments available in accessible formats.

14.3 Formal music performances

Formal music performances offer opportunities for pupils to develop their presentation skills and demonstrate their achievements. However, formal music performances introduce a range of additional challenges for pupils with visual impairment. Here are some of the challenges:

- sound checks and rehearsals in unfamiliar environments
- raised stress levels with limited opportunities for verbal explanation
- getting on and off the stage
- what to do in silent parts once on stage, before the performance and after the piece has finished
- using appropriate gesture and facial expression in performance to suit the style of music and size of venue
- following conductors' gestures.

Key action points

- The more organised and rehearsed the event is, the better – from off-stage to on-stage, through performing, bowing and leaving the stage.
- Keep instruments in the same relative position as in rehearsals.
- Discuss with the group how the sound is different in the performance area to the rehearsal space, perhaps getting a pupil to talk loudly whilst walking all around the edges of the room, giving some idea of the size.
- Walk and talk the performance space and discuss ways to get into position that pupils feel comfortable with.
- If using a sighted guide, make sure the guide is on the side away from the majority of the audience. If not using a sighted guide, experiment with trailing string or ribbon from a door handle to a chair or microphone stand centre stage. Have something to touch, such as the well of a grand piano, to check the angle to the audience is correct.
- Explain how to stand or sit on stage before the music begins, including standing still and having heads up.
- Rehearse posture in rests between verses in songs and in passages where other pupils are the focus of attention, particularly if this requires sitting down. This can be described in musical terms, e.g. after the piece count four beats in your head then all sit down.
- Rehearse how to start and end solo pieces, perhaps lifting up head before the start and lowering it after a silence at the end to show the audience can applaud. Rehearse how to acknowledge applause and then judge when to move off stage.
- Make sure pupils with visual impairment have a support assistant or a friend who can whisper an explanation of any change in plan.
- Getting on and off stage may be a good chance for pupils to practise sighted guide, good line walking, counting steps and noting sudden contrasts in lighting.

More dramatic entries that involve holding hands and skipping can be helpful for orientation and confidence.

- Rehearse facial expression and posture in rests in pieces, avoiding any mannerisms that do not fit in with the atmosphere of the music.
- Consider using dark glasses in intimate settings where other musicians might rely heavily on eye contact.

Resources

- Discuss recordings of live musicians with different musical styles, including Young Musician of the Year footage and Youth Music concerts.
- Musicians in Focus (www.musiciansinfocus.org) is an organisation that provides a central point of contact for the exchange and dissemination of information for musicians with visual impairment.

14.4 Using music technology independently

Music technology is increasingly becoming fundamental to music lessons. Pupils need to be able to use mainstream audio equipment such as CD players, karaoke machines and portable music players and, where appropriate, specialist recording and playback equipment such as DAISY, independently.

Computer packages aid composing and recording music; however, many music technology packages are visually detailed and fussy. Sighted pupils may approach music using a visual IT-based approach, whereas pupils with visual impairment may need to rely on their musical skills.

Key action points

- Find out what pupils already know and can do, and what packages they have on home equipment and any home or school device (laptop, memory stick, etc.).
- Encourage independent use of audio machines and orderly labelling and storage of recorded materials.
- Be aware of inexperienced pupils' limits on features of software packages, e.g. cutting and pasting.
- Ensure pupils have opportunities to check their work frequently by listening.
- Give pupils the opportunity to explore software away from the rest of the class, working at their own pace.
- Encourage teachers to consider all pupils' needs when selecting software to use in class.
- Ensure pupils are aware of the range of specialist audio and music equipment available to aid general study, and of the training available to use this effectively.
- When using live recording equipment, make sure pupils are aware of the whole package, not just the microphone at the end of the wire.

- Access recording equipment through tactile methods where necessary. Many mixing desks have click knobs for levels and a logical grid layout that is clear by touch given sufficient practice.

- Pupils may be able to access music scores through electronic formats confidently, e.g. MIDI, which may be a suitable way of presenting music whilst the rest of the class read print scores.

- Give pupils a chance to describe what they think is on the screen rather than describe it for them. Most of us use technology on a need-to-know and trial-and-error basis, rather than taking in lots of hypothetical possibilities explained to us.

- Try to limit mouse use by teaching key commands where available, and encourage pupils to keep adding to their own dictionary of key commands as they learn more.

- When using music technology for coursework for external qualifications, encourage students to keep a careful log, in a computer file, of imported materials and their manipulation for the descriptions needed by the examining bodies. Check current requirements for score production in composing units.

- Encourage pupils to create websites for their music and contribute to the music websites in school.

Resources

- Tacti Mark is a liquid plastic that when dabbed on, dries to produce raised permanent shapes, which are highly visible. This is useful for marking switches on CD players, etc. Available from RNIB in fluorescent orange, black and white.

- Expressive Software Projects (www.espmusic.co.uk) produces accessible educational music software.

- Widgit Software (www.widgit.com) produces educational software with emphasis on clear presentation.

- Search the internet for music shareware using search terms such as 'music shareware', 'music recorder' and 'music software'.

- Subscribe to a MIDI file music source such as www.prs.net

- The Drake Music Project (www.drakemusicproject.org) specialises in accessible music technology.

- Sibelius Speaking, using Jaws, is available for braillists from Dancing Dots (www.dancingdots.com). Dancing Dots also produces screen reading software for the sequencing package Sonar.

- Keep in touch with developments at www.musicatschool.co.uk

14.5 Assessing listening skills

Representing music through dance and artwork

Listening skills are often assessed by asking pupils to demonstrate visually what they hear through dance and movement, or through drawing and artwork. For pupils with visual impairment, describing what they hear can be difficult as visual language is often used, e.g. 'icy sounds'.

- Link pupils in movement activities, for example by holding a parachute as a whole group or using long fabric strips in groups and pairs.

- Use hands rather than whole body movement, with pupils touching fingertips and one leading the other in interpreting what is heard.

- Describe in words the link between the musical features and the type of movements used.

- Describe, and encourage pupils to describe, the whole gesture involved in a dance interpretation, including the speed and energy of the movement.

- Pupils could make up a story to describe the music rather than drawing a picture. This gives pupils the opportunity to link musical elements and structure to an extra-musical art form. Many young children are familiar with story tapes with musical background.

- Some pupils sit very still whilst listening attentively; do not misinterpret this as non-involvement!

- Try to keep background noise to a minimum when specifically listening to music to avoid other sounds, such as computer games, being interpreted as part of the music.

- Sounds can be more interesting if they move around and live sounds can be more interesting than recorded ones. Encourage much use of both!

Resources

- Use materials for dance props from local market stalls and shops.
- Have a wide variety of musical and other sound sources.
- Use story tapes and books with good-quality sound effects.

Accessing visual materials

Listening to music helps develop aural skills, which are particularly important for pupils with visual impairment. However, assessing pupils' listening skills often requires pupils to access visual materials so they can follow and describe the music. Pupils with visual impairment often do not have access to wall displays of musical instruments, types of music, etc., when asked to describe music and instruments. Pupils with visual impairment may also find following graphic and stave notation scores difficult whilst listening.

- Before undertaking a listening task, compile a list around the class of the elements to consider.

- Have on pupils' laptops a file in the music folder with a description of the wall displays in the room.

- Use tracking aids with score material, sometimes as simple as a ruler or a highlighter pen. The teacher can encourage all pupils to show they are following by using their fingers to track the score.

- Produce scores in accessible formats such as enlarged notation, modified stave notation, a graphic score with a continuous line to track, verbal description or braille music. This may require keeping to one line of music, rather than a score of many parts, so that only horizontal tracking is required, not vertical as well. Check with the music teacher what detail will not be needed in any modified version.

- Access music scores on computer packages that scroll the music, highlight what is playing, enlarge it and, in some cases, produce braille displays.

- Take care to spell out loud foreign and specialist terms, much used in music, and encourage pupils to keep a dictionary of special terms in their music records.

Resources

- Access music scores online, e.g. www.sibelius.com

- Produce assessment criteria in accessible formats.

- Use online musical dictionaries, including sites illustrating musical instruments and standard reference works for analysis.

14.6 Links between class music, extra-curricular music and music outside school

Pupils encounter music learning in a range of situations including class music, extra-curricular music and music outside school. Different adults involved in these activities, such as teachers, group leaders and other adults, including parents, may have different musical expectations and approaches. They may also have different experiences of working with pupils with visual impairment and different expectations about what different pupils can achieve. All adults should be encouraged to include pupils with visual impairment and be consistent in their expectations of pupils.

Key action points

- Encourage pupils to start instrumental lessons at a young age.

- Find out what musical activities pupils do outside school and inform the music teacher of these.

- Instrumental teachers working on a one-to-one basis with pupils may pick up all kinds of important information, feelings and capabilities, that could be useful in annual reviews, IEP target setting, etc.

- Encourage music leaders and instrumental teachers to talk to each other.

- Inform the instrumental teacher or group leader what can be done totally independently (such as the music), independently with warning (organising the taxi to come later after school), independently with specialist materials (ordering loan copies of the choir music in braille music) and with peer help (getting about during the break, getting on and off stage in performance).

- Instrumental teachers could teach braille music notation, as they are used to teaching stave notation in a way directly related to playing an instrument.

- One-to-one instrumental teachers working at an intermediate level or higher with a pupil using music notation may pick up deterioration in vision quickly, because of the complexity of reading and playing music.

- Access web listings of events in local music venues and community musical activities on a regular basis, checking out their access provision.

- Discuss memorising techniques with pupils, not only for learning the music but also for remembering what to practise, how to care for their instrument or voice, etc.

- Encourage pupils to be on time for rehearsals, learn music in time and ask, discreetly if necessary, when unsure of things.

- Check pupils know about instrument care and maintenance, and about insurance arrangements, where relevant.

- Discuss physical aspects of playing and carrying instruments discussing posture, muscle use and tension with pupils and teachers.

- For trips out and away, ensure that pupils have a buddy who is a peer and friend. Detach pupils from adults as much as possible; going away is getting away from all adults, not just parents!

- Encourage pupils to make a demonstration CD regularly to show their skills easily to new groups.

Resources

- Contact grade examination boards, such as ABRSM, Trinity Guildhall, Rock School, etc., for guidelines on access arrangements for external examinations.

- The music section of RNIB's website (www.rnib.org.uk/music) includes information on music events for people with visual impairment, awards and funding, braille and large print music, and accessible music technology.

For general enquiries on music issues for pupils with visual impairment, the RNIB Music Teachers' Support Group welcomes emails at mtsg@lists.rnib.org.uk

CHAPTER 15

Physical education

15.1 Running

Many teachers would consider running to be an extremely difficult, or even impossible, task for pupils with severe visual impairment. Fortunately, as with many activities, the challenges can be overcome with preparation, practice and some equipment.

Guide running

Pupils with severe visual impairment may be supported by an adult or a sighted pupil who acts as a guide and runs with the pupil. Contact is usually directly physical with younger pupils (hand hold or grasp above the elbow) and can progress to the use of a looped guide tether or rope.

Equipment
Choose a looped guide tether that is comfortable to both users. It should be fairly short and not stretchy. Pupils should run on an even surface with no obstacles to trip over.

Issues
- Ensure that the ability levels of the sighted guide and pupil with visual impairment are compatible.
- The sighted guide should not pull or lead the pupil with visual impairment, but should run at the pupil's pace. The guide and pupil with visual impairment should work together to develop skills for good safe co-running.
- Looped guide tethers and rope can slip so practise and experiment with different materials.
- Ensure that all runners have plenty of space. For safety, two lanes of a running track should be allocated to pairs of runners.
- Guide tethers and ropes give both runners more freedom to use their arms.
- In formal competitions, sighted guides must not cross the finish line first.
- With practice, sprint starts using blocks are possible with a sighted guide.
- Competition athletes who are officially categorised by British Blind Sport as B1 (totally blind) or B2 (partially blind) can run with a sighted guide in formal competitions.

Called running

An alternative to running with a sighted guide is 'called running': a sighted caller gives vocal instructions to a pupil with visual impairment. In formal competitions, this method is used only by B1 (totally blind) runners over a distance of 60 metres or less.

Equipment

- A loudhailer is sometimes used to amplify the voice.
- A running track with marked lanes is the ideal setting but this method is transferable to a field or similar.
- A B1 runner must wear a blindfold during formal competitions.

Method

- Competitors run one at a time and therefore compete against the clock.
- The runner is guided to the start line and placed in a central lane.
- The sighted caller stands on the track facing the runner.
- The caller faces the runner and stands some distance away, usually at a point beyond halfway.
- The caller repeatedly calls 'five' if the runner remains in a central position within the track or running area.
- If the runner drifts to the left, the signal 'four' is repeatedly called. If the runner drifts further to the left, the signal 'three' is called.
- If the runner drifts to the right, the signal 'six' is repeatedly called. If the runner drifts further to the right, the signal 'seven' is called.
- There should be constant voice contact between the runner and caller.

Issues

- The runner needs to have confidence in the vocal instructions, so plenty of practice is needed.
- Guide callers should know the runner and they should practise together.
- For safety reasons, there must be silence during the event. The caller must be alert to the possibility of external sound interference.
- The caller may need to run backwards.
- For safety reasons, the caller should be alert to the possibility that he/she may need to directly intervene in the runner's progress.

Resources

Contact British Blind Sport (www.britishblindsport.org.uk) for details of coaching, training and competition events.

15.2 Gymnastics

Opportunities and incentives to explore and experiment in activities involving climbing, swinging, hanging and balancing are often limited for pupils with visual impairment. As a consequence, body image and a desire to explore space may be underdeveloped. Equally, and understandably, a real fear of collisions and falls may be present. Gymnastics is an opportunity for pupils with visual impairment to experience challenges of exercising control over their bodies whilst expressing creativity in a safe environment.

Issues

- Allow time for tactile and spatial familiarisation of both apparatus and performing areas.
- Demonstrations should include accurate but short verbal descriptions.
- For safety and support, maintain verbal contact with pupils.
- Use a pupil's name prior to giving specific information.
- Equipment not in use should be stored in a designated area, out of the performing area.
- Contact and non-contact partner work are useful tools for learning. Pupils can use counting methods, as well as tactile and sound clues to work successfully with a partner.
- Sighted pupils mentally rehearse their movements; allow pupils with visual impairment to perhaps make a tactile route or to rehearse and hold a 'rhythm of movement' in their mind.

Floor work

- Pupils with visual impairment often have limited movement vocabulary. A supporting adult can play a key role in helping pupils to 'see' and understand how their bodies move.
- Transferring weight from one body part to another, exploring how the body can change shape and travel in different directions at differing speeds and linking simple actions together to make a short phrase of movement are all valid and exciting challenges.
- Teachers and support staff can use the sounds and rhythms of movement to give the feel of an action. Tactile stimuli, e.g. a ball for rounded shapes or a stick for long thin shapes, are useful aids to learning.
- Mats are useful as locators for movement and to absorb landings.
- Surfaces need to be safe and clean but also consider properties such as resistance, colour, lighting and sound, which affect how pupils use the space.
- Strong bright light may be a hazard to some pupils, especially those with albinism or photophobia.

Apparatus work

- Ensure that pupils with visual impairment have basic body management and self-control skills (possibly previously learned through floor work) prior to using apparatus.

- Progress through apparatus gradually, starting with low-level items such as benches, low box, low beams and then move on to medium-level equipment such as a movement table, beams and inclined benches, finishing with high-level apparatus.

- Words such as 'over', 'under', 'through', 'along' and 'around' encourage explorations of apparatus and of the spaces that are created by the apparatus.

- Pupils should always be barefoot as this gives much safer grip, strengthens the feet and assists balance.

- It is important for pupils to be able to land safely, especially when on high apparatus.

- Offer physical support as required, especially during balancing activities. Deciding when and how to reduce assistance is a judgement that comes with experience and patience and varies from one pupil to another.

15.3 Swimming

Swimming offers socially beneficial opportunities and pools are widely available. Pupils do not need technical equipment, nor are they necessarily dependent upon others for their involvement. Swimming can be an aid to developing body awareness, self-confidence and spatial orientation.

Issues

- All pupils must be aware of, and understand, the emergency procedures for clearing the pool and surrounding areas.

- To counter sound distortion, make verbal instructions and commands clear and brief. A supervising adult may need to use voice or tapping on a hard surface to give direction. Be aware that pupils with visual impairment may also have hearing impairment.

- When giving instructions, consider teacher positioning in relation to the group and pupils with visual impairment.

- Attendants should be alert to the potential for collisions between pupils, and the very real possibility of banging heads against the side of the pool.

- Be alert to the impact that bright light and water glare may have upon a pupil's orientation and performance.

- Pupils at risk of retinal detachment should not take part in activities such as diving. Discuss risks with a specialist teacher.

Key action points

- In the early stages, it is important to encourage general water play, e.g. paddling pools, water activity in the classroom. Early positive exposure to water and swimming activities helps to develop confidence and aids progression.

- In general, all standard age-appropriate activities are suitable. Activities using water toys, action rhymes, simple games and challenges, tactile stimuli and music are valuable aids to learning.

- Pupils should be made to feel secure in the water, whilst learning a healthy respect for the inherent dangers of water.

- Pupils may find it useful to walk or feel the dimensions and layout of the swimming area before the lesson. Similarly, counting strokes can help pupils to assess distances.

- A supporting adult should be prepared to enter the water to provide close guidance and support. Pupils will need to trust the supporting adult and the relationship between the two should be consistent, interactive, tailor-made for the individual and positive.

- Certificates and badges are very useful motivational tools. These can be designed in-house and presented for specific progress or achievements.

- Use lane ropes to separate swimmers and landmarks, such as steps and handrails, as directional locators. Floats wedged between walls and rails also provide useful marker points.

- Some pupils might be able to observe colour changes or landmarks within their environment, and use this information to assist them, for example, noting colour differences in lane ropes or counting beams in the ceiling.

Resources

- A tapper can be used to warn the pupil of the proximity of the end/side. A tapper is usually a mobility cane, or similar, with a sponge ball fixed to the end. Good use of a tapper needs practice between the pupil and supervisor.

- Prescription goggles are available from most opticians.

- Contact British Blind Sport (www.britishblindsport.org.uk) for details of coaching, training and competition events in swimming and other sports.

15.4 Team games

Pupils with visual impairment can take part in a range of team games, and many games can be adapted if necessary. Young children with visual impairment often require a lot of one-to-one experiential games play before they are ready to participate in team games. Skill levels, spatial and general awareness and emotional and social behavioural development can all be developed through physical activity and team games. However, at higher levels many physically demanding sports, such as rugby, may not be suitable for pupils with visual impairment and alternative activities might be required.

Issues

- The level of support provided to pupils with visual impairment affects progression. Too much support, and pupils become overly reliant and socially isolated; too little, and frustration and low self-esteem may result.

- Use a variety of sound clues in games activities to promote orientation awareness, and to inject an element of fun. Occasionally, sighted pupils could wear blindfolds or simulated spectacles to raise their awareness.

- All games that help pupils identify parts of their body, explore their environment and locate sounds are highly beneficial.

- Games can be invented that involve movement from one surface to another.

- Manipulative skills are frequently underdeveloped and therefore, physical activities using equipment are helpful in developing these skills.

- It is important to allow pupils the opportunity to explore the physical area and to feel the boundaries of play. Similarly, pupils should explore equipment before use. Mats are excellent for use as locators or boundaries. Large cones and gymnastic benches are also useful.

- Outdoor lessons can take advantage of natural features such as slopes, banks and pathway textures or grassed areas.

- Keep noise levels within safe limits. All pupils must be able to clearly hear instructions and remain in voice contact with the teacher.

- A sighted supporter within a large team game such as football should avoid dragging the pupil with visual impairment to keep pace with play. Instead, seek quality involvement, even if the game has to slow down momentarily.

- When playing ball games, verbal contact between recipient and sender helps all players prepare for action and achieve successful outcomes.

- Some eye conditions, such as a detached retina, may affect the suitability and safety of an activity. Always check with a specialist teacher before including pupils in activities.

- There are specifically adapted rules for blind cricket, and this allows all pupils with visual impairment to play equal parts.

- Use padding for goalposts, rugby posts, netball posts, etc. to protect all pupils.

Goalball

Goalball is a three-a-side team ball game developed for people with visual impairment but can be played with sighted people as well. Goalball has three main features that distinguish it from games played by sighted people: (i) the ball contains internal bells, which enable players to hear and locate it during play, (ii) the game is played on an indoor court or play area, with tactile markings to help players know where they are on court, (iii) all players wear eyeshades to ensure that everyone plays on an equal sight level.

Resources

- Contact British Blind Sport (www.britishblindsport.org.uk) for information on clubs and games fixtures.

- For more information on goalball, visit the British Blind Sport website or www.goalball.co.uk

- Sound balls are available in several sizes, colours, shapes and sounds from British Blind Sport.

- A range of accessible sports equipment, including goalballs, is available from Davies Sports (www.daviessports.co.uk).

- Padding for posts is available from Rhino Rugby (www.rhinorugby.com).

15.5 Outdoor and adventurous activities

Pupils with visual impairment are not usually drawn into adventurous play in the same way as their sighted peers; motivation and opportunity for spontaneous action is limited. On occasions, pupils are misguidedly protected from directly interacting with the world in which they live. Adults may think that involvement is too dangerous and discourage activity. In reality, pupils with visual impairment often need greater exposure, additional guidance and encouragement towards adventurous involvement.

Issues

- A major obstacle to participation is a lack of awareness of opportunities. Signage and literature at leisure centres, libraries or local press are likely to go unnoticed by pupils with visual impairment. Encourage pupils to ask about activities in their local area.

- Families, schools, colleges, residential settings, local clubs, national agencies, voluntary associations and health agencies may all need to be involved to enable positive accessible involvement in outdoor and adventurous activities for people with a range of access needs.

- Pupils with visual impairment may also have additional medical conditions such as cerebral palsy or epilepsy, and these will need to be considered when planning activity programmes.

Activities

- Orienteering tasks using tactile or sound clues, together with braille and large print clues, may all help pupils learn more about the environment and the task.

- Allow time for pupils to feel their environment; this is sometimes described as 'listening with the hands'. Fossils, grasses, rocks, roots and tree bark can all be explored. Similarly, standing on a mountain and feeling the strong wind on the face, or listening to the rush of a waterfall, are both exhilarating experiences.

- Any activity involving climbing, crawling, balancing, swinging or jumping is valuable for future challenges such as rock-climbing or negotiating assault courses.

- Pupils with severe visual impairment will need to be guided when negotiating obstacles. They may also need to be encouraged to use their hands, e.g. when feeling their way through a narrow space, or finding a handhold on a rock face.

- Pupils whose sight is better in daylight may require close support during evening or night-time activities.

- Learning to swim is not only desirable for safety reasons, but pupils who can swim are far more likely to seek and gain future involvement in a variety of water-based activities such as canoeing, water-skiing and sub-aqua diving.

- Roller skating promotes balance and can be taught indoors, and later pursued outdoors within a confined area or designated route. Pupils with no vision should be encouraged to use or make sounds to help them safely negotiate the area, but nevertheless they require constant supervision.

- Cycling is a useful activity and one that is easily continued through life. There is an enormous range of both standard and modified bikes, tricycles and tandems available. It may take time to learn and develop a pedalling technique. Fixed bikes and four-wheeled buggy cars are examples of useful starting points before progressing to cycling.

- Pupils with severe visual impairment often derive an enormous sense of freedom from tandem cycling. Membership of cycling clubs, or indeed any sports club, helps to form social links, promote physical activity and provide opportunities for raising self-esteem.

- Horse riding is a valuable activity, but often pupils have a fear of the horse. It is helpful to allow extra time to perhaps touch or groom the horse, feel the saddle, discuss apprehensions and to generally soak up the environment.

- Bouldering, which is simply feeling and exploring large rocks and boulders, is a natural precursor to rock climbing.

- Some challenges, such as potholing, may actually favour a beginner who is used to working with senses other than vision.

- An activity can be deemed successful if pupils have learned, enjoyed or experienced something new or memorable.

- Guides should be unobtrusive, communicative, knowledgeable and alert. They must be a help rather than a hindrance, and be aids to independence rather than promoters of dependence.

- Pupils without any vision sometimes find involvement easier than pupils who have to cope with fluctuating unpredictable eye conditions.

- Pupils with severe visual impairment may have little fear of heights, as they cannot see the distances involved and will not have a true concept of distance measurement. Similarly, distance judgement may be inaccurate when, for example, stepping from one point to another.

- Membership of sports clubs helps to form social links, promote physical activity and provide opportunities for raising self-esteem.

Resources

- Adventure games and activities can be introduced within the school environment. The gymnasium, hall, swimming pool and the school grounds are all suitable venues to learn the basics.
- Braille compasses are available from RNIB (www.rnib.org.uk) and UKGE Limited (www.ukge.co.uk).
- Braille and audio compasses, tactile maps and electronic guides are all excellent aids, but the presence of an experienced, qualified, sighted guide is vital.
- The Calvert Trust (www.calvert-trust.org.uk) specialises in outdoors activities for disabled people.
- The British Ski Club for the Disabled (www.bscd.org.uk) organises regular skiing trips to France for children and young people with visual impairment.

15.6 Dance

Positive dance experiences can enhance body image and body management skills and help develop balance, coordination and locomotion. Pupils who do not enjoy direct competitive events often prefer more personal activities such as dance, which may provide enhanced opportunities for personal development and self-confidence.

Issues

- Take time to describe other pupils' performances and allow time for pupils to experiment and share their ideas.
- Modern dance offers freedom of choice of movements, but remember this freedom can be daunting to pupils with visual impairment. Give clear instructions and feedback.
- Demonstrate movements with physical contact; move with the pupil.
- Be alert to the potential for accidental bumps when pupils are moving around, particularly at speed, when changing direction or at differing levels.
- Pupils with visual impairment need to be taught how to land safely when jumping. Pupils should have the opportunity to discover how deeply they should bend their knees, and which actions naturally follow a landing.
- Pupils who have never seen often have a limited understanding of stretching; often their efforts lack tension and awareness.
- Simple action rhymes are ideal for early learners. They help to develop an awareness of body parts, and encourage independent movement and a sense of rhythm.
- Use sounds, poems, prose, weather, emotions, seasons and events as stimuli.
- Tapping out rhythms on the floor, body or an item of equipment are all good ways to develop a sense of rhythm and timing.
- Working in pairs or groups offers a wealth of movement possibilities. For example, pupils may devise sequences to demonstrate paired shapes or to travel whilst keeping partner contact.

- Structured movement within national dance or line dancing can provide security for pupils who are not confident working independently.

- Build up an understanding of simple movement words such as 'forward', 'backward', 'sideways', 'high', 'low', 'up', 'down', 'left', 'right', 'narrow', 'wide', 'stretched' and 'curled'.

Equipment

- Handling different materials and exploring their texture, size and shape can prove useful aids to interpretation and understanding, and helps encourage expressive movement. For example, feeling a round soft ball may help a pupil to understand, and perhaps adopt and travel in a tucked curved shape.

- Establish well-defined areas for activity, with non-slip surfaces that are large enough to support the performances.

- Movement body bags can help pupils feel the dynamics of their actions. For example, when stretching, pupils can feel the resulting tensions between their action and the fabric. Equally, the abstract nature has the potential to de-personalise a performance, and perhaps give a degree of anonymity to a self-conscious pupil. Suppliers include Davies Sports (www.daviessports.co.uk).

- Elastic rings are good for group work as they provide a tactile link and a starting point for movement.

CHAPTER 16

Science

16.1 Accessible equipment

Science equipment can either be modified for use by pupils with visual impairment or specialist equipment can be purchased. Discuss with pupils what works for them and then transfer the information into new situations. Here are some ideas for accessible science equipment.

Keeping things orderly and making equipment more visible

- Place all equipment for an experiment in a tray. This will allow pupils to locate items quickly and efficiently. Many pupils find carrying out an experiment within the confines of a tray very helpful, as there is less chance of losing a vital piece of equipment at the crucial moment.

- Use brightly coloured equipment in contrasting colours where possible. Use brightly coloured paint to colour equipment edges.

Scales

Choose equipment carefully; search for equipment with highly visible scales. Use plastic measuring cylinders with raised scales and numbers.

- When you find equipment that really suits a pupil, buy some extra pieces and keep them in stock.

- Mark scales on equipment using large print and braille labels.

- Use Wikki Stix or plastic dots made from Tacti Mark, a brightly coloured liquid plastic that hardens to form a tactile mark, to make highly visible and tactile markings on equipment.

- Tactile and high-visibility metre rulers and tactile tape measures are available. Standard tape measures can be marked by sticking plastic strips to the scale.

- String can be knotted at known distances apart and painted bright colours to provide a cheap measuring string.

Measuring out small volumes

Use a sharp knife or scalpel to make notches in syringe plungers to help pupils to feel when the correct volume has been drawn up.

Models

- There are lots of models available from scientific suppliers and some are excellent as they are highly coloured and have a variety of textures.

- Add labels in large print or braille using sticky-back plastic or Dymo tape.

- Use visits from sales representatives and trips to exhibitions to investigate the best buys for your purposes.

- Some laboratory technicians have a talent for making models that work better than those available from standard suppliers.

Data-logging

Data-logging is an area of current expansion. The software supplied with data-logging equipment often has the facility to provide an enlarged meter on the screen. It is worth investigating whether speech software can access these numbers to provide a range of talking devices such as voltmeters, ammeters and oxygen meters. The printout from these programs can often be modified to provide enlarged and tactile graphs without too much effort.

Light probes and colour detectors

- Light probes indicate the presence of light by a change in audio or tactile output.

- A passive light probe reacts to external light sources, and is useful for detecting if electric lights are switched on, e.g. on cookers or computer equipment.

- An active light probe sends out a visible beam of light that is reflected back to the probe's sensor to measure different levels of reflected light. Active light probes can be used for detecting the liquid level in beakers, etc., and detecting printed text on paper.

- Colour detectors are small hand-held devices that use speech output to identify colours.

Diagrams

- Make large print or tactile versions of posters of equipment, flashcards, etc.

- The SEN section of the Association for Science Education website (www.ase.org.uk/sen) has a range of free resources to download, including vocabulary flashcards with large print diagrams, a range of focus activities and a diagram maker, which is an interactive tool for producing diagrams of equipment and experiments.

Resources

- RNIB (www.rnib.org.uk) supplies a range of specialist equipment, including Dymo guns for making braille labels, Wikki Stix, Tacti Mark, tactile and high-visibility metre rulers and tape measures and audio and vibrating light probes.

- A talking colour detector is available from Cobolt Systems Ltd (www.cobolt.co.uk).

16.2 Microscope work: Revealing the invisible to all

A microscope adapted for use with a video camera and monitor can enable pupils with visual impairment to take part in and benefit from microscope activities. Sighted pupils can also benefit from this method.

Equipment

You will need a microscope adapted for use with a video camera and monitor. The monitor can be a television screen or a computer monitor. Video microscopes are available from Philip Harris (www.philipharris.co.uk) and Brunel Microscopes Ltd. (www.brunelmicroscopes.co.uk).

Accessing the image

Drawing on the monitor screen with a black water-soluble pen can help pupils locate the important features. You can also place drawing film onto the screen and trace around the image. You could then use this film to make a tactile diagram for pupils who are unable to access the image through sight.

Measuring

To calculate the magnification of the microscope and video camera system, place a transparent plastic ruler onto the stage of the microscope and measure the image on the monitor screen. Divide this measurement by the actual measurement to give the magnification. Remember, the magnification by the video camera and monitor makes the image larger, but does not increase the definition of the image.

Recording

One advantage of using a video camera system is that the images can be recorded for future use. You can also use computers and digital cameras to capture microscope images, enhance them and keep them for future reference. Most pupils with visual impairment cannot draw diagrams to a high enough standard for assessment. But they can label diagrams that have been prepared in advance and annotate them.

More information

For further specialist advice on this topic, see the article on microscopy at www.rnibnewcollege.worcs.sch.uk (follow the links in the Outreach section).

16.3 Heating things safely

Good health and safety practice is vital for heating things safely. Heating is essential to the science class and pupils who are not allowed to heat because of health and safety issues feel excluded from the lesson. Include all pupils by planning the lesson and putting measures in place so that accidents are unlikely to happen. Consider what accidents might happen and how you would manage them. Write down this risk assessment.

Preventing accidents

- When planning an experiment consider the temperature required. For most experiments in chemistry, temperatures well over 100°C are needed and a Bunsen burner is used. However, many experiments require temperatures below 100°C. A water bath or hot plate can be used instead of a Bunsen burner in these cases.

- Paint the tops of equipment such as tripods, beakers and Bunsen burners with a bright heat-resistant paint to make them more visible. Always place a bench mat under the hot plate so that the area of danger is more visible. The bench mat can also be painted a contrasting colour.

- Pupils with no sight may locate roaring Bunsen flames by sound. Objects passed through the flame change the noise made by the flame. Use the edge of the tripod as a guide rail when heating objects directly in the Bunsen flame.

- Teach pupils to follow a set procedure for placing a test tube into a water bath. The following procedure works well for partially sighted pupils as well as for those with no sight. Teach the pupil to hold the test tube in their favoured hand. Use the other hand to slide over the laboratory bench and find the bench mat. Then find the base of the tripod, water bath or hot plate. Make sure that their hand stays on the surface of the bench, as the danger is higher than the bench surface. Now use the test tube as a cane to tap their way up to the entry of the heating container and finally into the container. Some pupils will need a support worker's help to practise this. Guide pupils' hands, with pupils' permission, for the first few tries to give them confidence.

- Some pupils will eventually have sufficient confidence to learn the height of the test tube in the heating container and be able to remove it to a test tube rack. The key is to realise that the thickened glass at the top of a test tube is always at a lower temperature than the rest of the tube. Supervision should always be given when pupils are handling hot objects.

- Many of the protocols that require strong heating start with cold apparatus. This is a stage that can include pupils with visual impairment without risk. With supervision it is possible to allow pupils to lift the lid on a crucible.

Resources

Safety goggles that fit over prescription spectacles are widely available.

16.4 Mini beasts

Studying mini beasts can be a very difficult subject for pupils with visual impairment, as mini beasts cannot easily be experienced through touch or without magnification.

- Some mini beasts can be handled successfully (taking all health and safety issues into account, and observing guidelines for the study and care of mini beasts and their natural habitats). Although handling and keeping mini beasts is sometimes discouraged, it may be the only way pupils with visual impairment can have equality of access. Some of the best subjects include snails, spiders, caterpillars (check the species), ladybirds, worms and frogs.

- Snails can be kept successfully in a tank, and pupils with visual impairment can monitor their progress, e.g. shell growth, amount of plants eaten, etc. Snails will also respond well to some handling and pupils with no vision often appear to enjoy feeling them, possibly as there is no pre-conception of what slime looks like. Snails can even be listened to, as they make quite a noise when eating!

- The life cycle of a frog, and of different types of frogs, can be well illustrated using models available from educational suppliers and toyshops.

- Butterfly models with paper wings are available from science sections of educational catalogues; some realistic butterfly models are available from many accessory shops as fashion items. All of these make the life cycle of the butterfly easy to access through tactile methods. For younger pupils the book *The Very Hungry Caterpillar* by Eric Carle can be very successfully adapted into tactile or large print formats.

- Tactile diagrammatic life-cycles can be successfully made using heat swell paper. Do not make the diagrams too wide and ensure that each picture is no more than 5cm; otherwise the diagram as a whole becomes too complicated to follow.

- Many mini beasts can be observed using a video magnifier. Put live mini beasts in a Petri dish to keep them within focus, and return them to their habitat as soon as possible. Sometimes dead mini beasts can be found naturally, and can be kept in small airtight containers for magnified observation. Dead bees are also large enough to be felt by pupils with visual impairment.

- Surprisingly realistic models of flies are available from joke shops!

- Spiders are one of the most successful mini beasts for pupils with visual impairment to study. Live spiders can be experienced if allowed to crawl on hands or, even better, arms (the sensation is magnified by the hairs on the arms). Realistic models are available from a number of sources, especially at Halloween, a good time to stock up! Real spiders' webs can be felt carefully; they are very strong and quite sticky, and pupils respond well to exploring them. They are also more easily found in the environment than other habitats (outer windowsills are often good sources).

  To explore web patterns, three-dimensional rubber spiders' webs make better illustrations than tactile pictures; likewise fake web material (as used in film props) is available from joke and novelty shops and can be stretched and spread between obstacles by all pupils.

16.5 Microbiology

Microbiology is studied throughout the secondary school curriculum. The major issues for inclusion of pupils with visual impairment in microbiology lessons are health and safety ones, and for this reason the emphasis in this topic is on practical safe working practices.

Choosing organisms

- Choose safe microorganisms that grow well at temperatures between 25°C and 30°C. This reduces the risk of growing pathogenic contaminants.
- Try to choose at least one organism that produces coloured colonies. *Micrococcus luteus* produces yellow colonies on nutrient agar. This makes the colonies more accessible to pupils with visual impairment.
- A light probe can detect a colony, but it works better if the colony is coloured.
- Place Petri dishes on a light box and mark colonies using a black felt-tip pen.

Sterile techniques

- Many of the actions involved in sterile techniques involve passing objects through a Bunsen flame. Pupils should practise these techniques as well as those involving the accurate measuring of liquids.
- Demonstrate techniques by getting pupils to follow your hands as you demonstrate and then guide their hands as they make their first attempts. Later, some pupils will develop sufficient skill to work independently but there should always be a responsible person close by ready to intervene should the pupil lose their place and start to put themselves in danger.

Resources

- CLEAPSS School Science Service (www.cleapss.org.uk) produces useful lists and advice sheets, which include lists of safe bacteria and culture information.
- The National Centre for Biotechnological Education (www.ncbe.reading.ac.uk) has developed a number of useful aids for teaching microbiology; the website is also full of really good advice.

16.6 Genetics

The two major issues for inclusion of pupils with visual impairment in genetics lessons are choosing suitable materials for practical work and presenting solutions to genetics problems.

Materials

- Choose genetic traits that are accessible to pupils with little or no sight.
- Use plants that have non-visual characteristics, for example:
  - choose plants that show dwarf and non-dwarf characteristics; maize is a good choice
  - use a light probe to compare white plants from seedlings with wild green plants

- choose plants with different leaf shapes; hairs and coloured stems are difficult to identify
- use taste to identify the presence or absence of cucurbitacin in cucumber plants; however, some pupils seem to be unable to taste the bitter taste.

Presenting solutions to genetic questions

- Family trees can be difficult for pupils to read. Ensure the symbols are clear and have good contrast, e.g. squares and triangles for sex and black and white shades for phenotypes, or filled and non-filled shapes with braille users.
- Classical solutions to Mendelian crosses are best solved using the punnet-square method rather than family-tree diagrams with lots of crossing lines. The punnet square combines the alleles produced by each parent to give all the possible combinations to produce the offspring. Avoid diamond-shaped tables; use simple rows and columns as shown below.

Table 16.1   Punnet square for a cross involving one gene with two characteristics or alleles

Gametes	A	a
A	AA	Aa
a	Aa	aa

- The science braille code contains a detailed section on how to lay out solutions to problems in genetics. The layouts are identical to the ones that are often found in good biology textbooks. This means that all pupils are solving the problem in the same way so no one should feel excluded.
- For braille users, use the dot 6 capital-letter sign in front of the upper-case letters and use the dot 5 6 letter sign in front of the lower-case letters. To save space, miss out the 5 6 letter sign in front of the capital-letter sign.
- In print and braille, simplify the symbols used for blood groups and the superscript system for identifying genes used in fruit fly genetics to simple upper- and lower-case letters.

16.7 Electrical circuits

The usual approach to teaching circuits is to create interesting models, e.g. making a lighthouse work. Although this can be fun, the models are often complicated and they can be difficult for pupils with visual impairment to understand. So, to ensure inclusion, basic models are best. Pupils using print can usually draw symbols and circuit diagrams after the hands-on activities described below, although they may have trouble ending the wires accurately at the edge of the symbols.

Real objects

- Use real objects to introduce basic circuits; introduce a cell and a buzzer then gradually move on to more complicated circuits with switches and more cells.

- Pupils with visual impairment understand more quickly if a buzzer is used instead of a bulb. Bulbs can be introduced when pupils are familiar with circuits.

- If possible, mount circuits on a baseboard. This stops too much tangling of wires and, because objects are held still, it makes it easier for pupils to attach clips to cells, etc. The circuit can also be moved about much more easily.

- Crocodile clips are often easiest for pupils with visual impairment to manipulate.

Tactile diagrams

- Introduce tactile circuit symbols to braille users and pupils with severe visual impairment using heat swell paper. The symbols should not be too large (about 1–2cm) so the whole item is felt easily with a fingertip (see also 4.4 Tactile diagrams).

- Symbols on cards can be used for matching activities and for identifying and labelling real circuits. Eventually pupils will need to recognise diagrams of circuits, and these are best presented on heat swell paper.

- Drawing circuits, e.g. on drawing film, is a very difficult skill for pupils with visual impairment and is not really necessary. If pupils can recognise symbols and diagrams, it is more useful to do matching activities, choosing the correct diagram from four examples, etc.

16.8 Sounds

Most sound experiments can be easily adapted for pupils with visual impairment. Consider using blindfolds with sighted pupils to encourage all pupils to use their hearing only.

Ideas for experiments

- Exploring vibrations – use rice, peas, beads, etc. on a drum. Use a drum with a raised edge. The size and amount of items used, the size of the drum and strength of the hit will create different movements. Pupils can feel the movement of the rice, etc., by holding their hand just above the drum skin so that the rice, etc. jumps up to them. They often need help to keep their hand steady, and need to repeat the experience a number of times.

- Sound travelling through solids – rest an ear on a table to hear and feel vibrations travel through the solid. Use different sizes of table, made with various materials, and bang on them with various objects.

- Sound travelling through solids – go into an adjoining room and bang on the wall. Pupils will probably never have focused on the fact that sound is travelling through a solid when they hear noises from other rooms. Pupils can also rest an ear on the wall to feel vibrations. This exercise is very good for promoting spatial awareness; pupils with visual impairment may not have realised that another room is on the other side of a wall.

- Sound travelling through air – use a bell, whistle, maraca, etc. in an open space at various distances from pupils, and let them notice how it gets louder as it gets closer. Even though pupils with visual impairment can't see how far away the person with the bell is, this experiment reinforces understanding of distance as well as sound travel.

- Pitch experiments – all pupils can experience pitch experiments in the same way, e.g. by plucking strings, changing pitch of drums, etc. Always allow pupils with visual impairment to experience the vibrations as well, and let them have hands-on contact with the experiment rather than just listening; they need to experience how the sound is being produced.

  Pupils often enjoy altering pitch using a plastic ruler on the edge of a table; it produces vibrations and sound through a kinaesthetic experience. They also like the fact that it is not a musical instrument creating the sound.

- Tuning fork experiments are recommended.

- Plastic cup and string telephone experiment – make sure the people at each end are in different rooms; otherwise pupils may assume they are hearing the voice normally. This experiment links sound with spatial and distance awareness.

- Experiments using real sounds are preferable to experiments using electronically produced sounds.

16.9 Shadows

Initially the concept of shadows appears to be difficult for pupils with visual impairment. However, shadows can be taught effectively as shown below and should involve actual experiences where possible.

Shade

Link the idea of shadows to pupils' experiences of shade. Pupils will have noticed shade by a tree, next to a building, etc. Draw on these experiences to explain what shadows are and how they happen.

  Pupils with visual impairment need to understand words such as 'transparent' and 'opaque' to fully understand why shadows occur. Link explanations of these to their experiences of the Sun's warmth coming through a window, but not through a wall or door. Ask, 'On a sunny day what do you feel when you stand under a sunshade or umbrella, compared with no shade?'

Shape

The shape of shadows is more difficult to understand. The experiment of a light source projected past an opaque shape onto a wall can work well. A projector is the strongest and best light source, but a torch or lamp can be used if a projector is not available.

Make sure the opaque shape has a very clear and definite outline: a basic wooden or plastic puppet or figure, a presentation plaque or even a table tennis bat will all work well.

Project light onto a large sheet of card and draw around the shadow. Cut out the shadow's shape. Pupils with visual impairment can then feel and hold the shadow.

Extend the experiment by moving the light source or object closer and further away (depending on the results needed) and cut out the shadow shapes. The different sizes of the tactile shadows can then be compared. Don't forget to label each cut-out with the relevant part of the experiment. For fun, use this technique to make silhouettes of different people, and let pupils compare them.

Movement of the Sun

Exploring the movement of the Sun and its effect on shadows is not easy, but it is possible. Following the movement of the shadow over time is easier to understand than following the changing length and width of the shadow.

To measure the movement and length of shadows outside over a period of time, use a pole on a stand and replace chalk lines with lengths of string, secured at the furthest end with sticky putty or Plasticene, which will stick to tarmac for a number of hours as long as it doesn't rain, or isn't too windy (wind lifts the string). Choose the surface for the experiment carefully; concrete, tarmac or wood are suitable for this experiment, but grass isn't. Even more substantial than string is thin dowelling cut to the different lengths.

To compare the widths of the shadows as they elongate and shorten, record measurements with rulers or tapes; or cut widths of card for tactile comparisons. For pupils with severe visual impairment, use a light probe to locate the shadows (see 16.1 Accessible equipment).

16.10 Reflection, refraction and colour

Reflection, refraction and colour are difficult concepts for pupils with severe visual impairment, but worth pursuing. To pupils with visual impairment, colours are adjectives used to describe all sorts of things. We refer to red as being a warm colour and blue as a cold colour, we refer to yellow as cheerful and green for jealousy. Teach pupils how coloured objects react in different light conditions; it also helps with colour coordination when choosing clothes.

Key action points

- Start with simple concepts such as shadows.

- Use ray boxes and combs to produce parallel, convergent and divergent rays. Use a light probe to investigate the position and direction of the rays. Encourage pupils to move the probe slowly. Cover the surface with sheets of white paper and use black felt-tip pens to mark the position of the rays. The sheets can then be used to produce raised diagrams on swell paper. Cork graph boards or cork tiles with pins and elastic bands can also be used to trace the rays. Have suitable raised and print diagrams for pupils to examine.

- Introduce mirrors and prisms to investigate the laws of reflection and refraction. Creating diagrams using felt pens, pins and elastic bands will allow angles to be measured using tactile and large print protractors.

- Refraction produces the rainbow and the light probe can discriminate between the different colours in a bright spectrum. It is worth taking the time to ensure that a good example can be produced during the lesson. It adds interest if the spectrum can be arranged to fall onto one of the pupils. Quite a nice tactic is to have the spectrum fall on a chosen pupil's clothing. The class can then examine the spectrum produced on the living screen.

  If stage spotlights are available, colour mixing can be done on a large scale and effects of different coloured lights falling on different coloured materials can be investigated in the context of theatre productions.

Resources

There is a more detailed article on this topic by Norman Brown in *Curriculum Close-Up* No.19, which is available from RNIB's Curriculum Information Service (www.rnib.org.uk/curriculum).

CHAPTER 17

Additional subjects

17.1 Drama

What are the challenges of acting for young people with visual impairment, and how do we overcome them?

The script

The greatest challenge is exactly the same as it is for all pupils – encouraging pupils to learn their words so that they are not left with an overwhelming task in the last couple of weeks before the performance. However, this task is often more challenging for pupils with visual impairment, as a small copy of a play that can be held in one hand is much easier to act around than a braille or large print script that needs to be held close to the face. It is difficult to do more than read aloud the words when burdened with a bulky script. Some pupils with visual impairment may find it easier to learn lines from an audio recording than from print or braille. After words are learned, pupils can start to think about using their hands for expression, making eye contact and moving around.

The set

Consider pupils with visual impairment at the planning stage of the set. Orientation clues should be built into the design, so that actors can use the set itself to further develop their performances. Use a change of texture or objects to mark a tactile line near the front of the stage. Pupils can use this firstly to work out how close they are to the audience, and secondly to find items such as chairs, tables, etc., which can be placed along the line.

The action

Building an accessible set and learning the lines are two of the biggest barriers for presenting a performance including pupils with visual impairment. Additional mobility challenges usually vary enormously from production to production. A memorable example from a production at a specialist school for pupils with visual impairment is the axe murder scene in *Little Shop of Horrors* (Ashman and Menken 1982), when the actor holding the axe was totally blind. This was solved by filming it in advance, in silhouette. The 'victim' very bravely stood nearby while the murderer chopped with the axe at a box. Another example at the same school was the cliff rescue scene in *Our Day Out* (Russell 1977), which was choreographed through discussion with the two actors and then practised safely until both were certain about what each would do and when.

Gesture and expression

Pupils with very little or no vision at all often need support in developing appropriate facial expressions, or arm gestures such as a point, wave or inverted commas drawn in the air. These can be described or modelled for pupils to feel, or pupils can be shown how to perform the action themselves. Discuss the methods with pupils and use whichever method they find most effective and are comfortable with.

Review

Overall, the challenges faced by pupils with visual impairment differ only slightly from those faced by all pupils. Experience has shown that pupils' motivation, teamwork, willingness to go a little bit further and creativity make the commitment of time and effort in putting on a production thoroughly worthwhile.

17.2 Religious education

It is important to understand pupils' visual impairment and associated implications within the classroom setting before thinking about the stimulating environment that can be provided through religious education. It is essential that a specialist teacher has completed a full functional vision assessment, which will detail teaching approaches, seating position, lighting, use of audio, etc. (see 5.3 Assessment of functional vision).

An accessible atmosphere and environment for religious education

To create an atmosphere of awe and wonder, which is so much a part of religious education, some small adaptations can be made to the classroom environment.

- Bright wall displays should be accessible at an appropriate eye level (or hand level for tactile displays), and should be uncluttered and clearly labelled, with artefacts easily available.

- Arrange artefacts near to wall displays to encourage independent learning strategies and concepts, which can then be revisited using real experiences. A display describing a world religion solely in lengthy text with accompanying illustrations will have little impact on pupils with visual impairment. However, a display using clear bold text, posters and artefacts will have greater meaning and purpose.

- Displays should be hands on wherever possible. Any text should be written in a left to right orientation to avoid visual confusion, which in turn can cause meaning to be lost.

Use of language in religious education

- Use of language when teaching religious education to pupils with visual impairment is very important. It is easy to take for granted the use of pictures and other visual stimuli in day-to-day teaching. These can be attractive to look at, a useful tool to encourage a stimulating environment and help to explain concepts, but such visual tools do not necessarily help pupils with poor vision.

- Never assume that pupils with visual impairment have understood a concept immediately, as so much incidental learning will have been lost. Pupils may not be familiar with places of worship and religious symbols.

- Take time to repeat information, describe, share ideas verbally and encourage oral expression by all whenever possible.

- Audio resources are useful when teaching religious education, as passages from religious texts can be difficult to find and scan and also difficult to visually focus upon.

- Remember that pupils with visual impairment often process information at a slower rate than sighted pupils. Teachers' language should encourage pupils to extract meaning from what is presented verbally, rather than relying solely on visual information. Language should not be vague; it should be clear and precise.

Resources

Adapt textbooks and worksheets to meet the criteria set out in pupils' functional visual assessments. Materials should also be differentiated if necessary by removing clutter and unnecessary illustrations. This will enable pupils to access the scheme of work efficiently and effectively alongside their fully sighted peers (see 4.5 Modifying learning resource materials).

Some religious texts are available in braille, large print and audio formats (see 18.3 Obtaining accessible learning resource materials).

17.3 Accessible assemblies

Use of language

As with all classroom-based teaching, ensure that language is clear, concise and well defined. A well-planned assembly maintains this consistent approach to language. Pupils with visual impairment often depend on language in assemblies, as they are unable to see information on whiteboards, etc.

What to avoid?

Avoid presenting information through visual media only, e.g. whiteboards, overhead projectors, posters and other visual stimuli. Pupils with visual impairment may feel isolated, bored and unaware of what is being presented. Where appropriate, give pupils individual copies of materials presented visually.

Good practice in presenting an assembly

Always read aloud information presented on whiteboards, posters, etc. Show pictures, e.g. of religious artefacts, but then, if possible have the real items ready to pass to pupils (depending on the size of the assembly). When seeking answers to questions, always address pupils by name rather than pointing.

Use of music is an excellent way of capturing the attention of all pupils. Taste, touch and sense of smell can be incorporated into any assembly for all pupils, where appropriate. With careful planning and imagination, assemblies can be accessible by all.

17.4 Personal, Health and Social Education

Personal, Health and Social Education (PHSE) offers pupils the opportunity to engage in discussion with less dependence on visually presented materials than many other subjects. However, although vision may not be directly used during discussion, there are considerations about participation and, crucially, the ways in which the experiences of pupils with visual impairment differ from those of their peers.

Participation in discussion

In class discussion, pupils are often required to put up a hand before speaking. When discussion is in small groups, pupils usually rely on subtle visual signals from others to judge the appropriate time to express their own views. Pupils with visual impairment may need cueing in, and may benefit from a 'one speaker at a time' rule.

Using video

Pupils with visual impairment may benefit from the opportunity to view a video before it is shown in class, maybe by taking it home a few days in advance. This will provide the opportunity to sit as close as is necessary without blocking the view of others. Pupils will then be able to participate more fully in the follow-up classwork. As far as possible, select videos that do not rely exclusively on visual images. If there is no alternative, it may be necessary to provide audio description for pupils with severe visual impairment.

Visual experience

It is easy to assume that the whole class will have common experiences, particularly in everyday matters such as going out with friends or watching popular television programmes. Pupils with severe visual impairment may not have this level of independence; these pupils may spend more time with adults than with their peers. Television may be enjoyed for the dialogue rather than the pictures. Avoid assumptions that experiences are common to all.

Outside speakers

It is important to inform visiting speakers well in advance of the specific needs of all pupils. If it is not possible for the speaker to adapt material appropriately, the school may need to provide additional support or liaise with the speaker so that any modifications can be made in advance.

Disability awareness

The PHSE curriculum can provide excellent opportunities for increasing disability awareness in general. This may be addressed on a class basis or as a whole-year group activity. This can be extremely successful if the local support service can be persuaded to participate and provide activities that will increase the understanding of the challenges faced by pupils with disabilities and the ways in which these challenges may be met.

Conclusion

Keep in mind pupils' different life experiences and use these experiences to broaden the horizons of others.

Resources and glossary

CHAPTER 18

Equipment and resources

A range of equipment and resources has been mentioned within the chapters of this book. This chapter provides supplier details for independent living aids, access technology and accessible education resources and a list of materials provided on the accompanying CD. This chapter also contains information on obtaining braille, large print, Moon and audio learning resource materials, and a list of useful organisations and websites that provide information and advice on issues relating to visual impairment.

Local authority sensory support services

It is recommended that the first point of contact for any help regarding equipment and resources should be the local authority sensory support service. They may already have a supply of equipment and resources available for pupils with visual impairment.

18.1 Directory of suppliers

Independent living aids and access technology

AccessABLE World supplies a range of products for people with visual impairment, including braille software, the Book Courier audio player, high-visibility playing cards, large print and audio calculators, a liquid level indicator, screen reader software, screen magnifier software, talking dictionaries, talking personal organisers, a talking tape measure and a range of task lighting.

- Website: www.accessableworld.com
- Telephone: 0870 321 7099 within the UK or +44 (0) 1689 833123 outside the UK
- Email: sales@accessableworld.com

Adapt-IT supplies a range of equipment and computer aids including braille embossers, braille displays, braille and large print keyboards, braille software, read and scan software and stand-alone scanners, screen reader software, screen magnifier software and video magnifiers.

- Website: www.adapt-it.org.uk

- Telephone: +44 (0) 845 644 1712
- Email: info@adapt-it.org.uk

Aspire Consultancy provides a range of access technology including braille displays, braille embossers, keyboards, screen readers, screen magnifiers, scanning software and video magnifiers.

- Website: www.aspire-consultancy.co.uk
- Telephone: +44 (0) 1904 762788
- Email: info@aspire-consultancy.co.uk

Blazie supplies a range of access technology including braille displays, braille embossers, braille software, electronic notetakers, scanning software and video magnifiers.

- Website: www.blazie.co.uk
- Telephone: +44 (0) 20 8582 0450
- Email: barry.webb@blazie.co.uk

Cobolt Systems Ltd specialises in aids for people with visual impairment, including talking calculators, talking colour detector, talking kitchen scales, talking labels, talking liquid level indicator, talking microwave oven, talking time switch and a talking tape measure.

- Website: www.cobolt.co.uk
- Telephone: +44 (0) 1493 700172
- Email: cobolt@compuserve.com

CR Clarke supplies vacuum-forming machines (thermoform) and vacuum-forming sheets in a range of colours.

- Website: www.crclarke.co.uk
- Telephone: +44 (0) 1269 590530
- Email: info@crclarke.co.uk

Disability Supplies has an online catalogue of independent living aids designed for people with a range of needs, including visual impairment. Products include canes, writing guides, Bumpons, highly visible adhesive tape, large print and braille playing cards, liquid level indicator and talking scales.

- Website: www.disabilitysupplies.co.uk
- Telephone: +44 (0) 1342 837691
- Email: sales@disabilitysupplies.co.uk

Dycem supplies a range of highly visible non-slip products, which are useful for providing contrast and preventing equipment from slipping.

- Website: www.dycem.com
- Telephone: +44 (0) 117 9559921
- Email: uk@dycem.com

Force 10 supplies a range of products for people with visual impairment, including braille keyboards, braille notetakers, IVEO™ touch pad and software for audio tactile diagrams, large print and talking calculators, screen reader software, scanning software, screen magnifier software, Tiger embossers, hand-held video magnifiers and stand-alone video magnifiers.

- Website: www.forcetenco.co.uk
- Telephone: +44 (0) 1372 450887
- Email: sales@forcetenco.co.uk

IC-Online Ltd supplies a range of products for people with visual impairment, including Bumpons, an automatic needle threader, large print games and puzzles, large print keyboards, liquid level indicators, non-slip mats, tactile marking paste, talking kitchen scales, a talking measuring jug, a talking microwave oven, talking thermometers, task lighting and a wide range of magnifiers.

- Website: www.ic-online.co.uk
- Telephone: +44 (0) 1457 819790
- Email: sales@IC-Online.co.uk

Inclusive Technology supplies a range of software and hardware products for people with a range of needs, including large print keyboards, screen magnifiers and screen readers.

- Website: www.inclusive.co.uk
- Telephone: +44 (0) 1457 819790
- Email: inclusive@inclusive.co.uk

New Vision Technology supplies a wide range of video magnifiers.

- Website: www.newvisiontechnology.com
- Telephone: +44 (0) 1249 814309
- Email: info@newvisiontechnology.com

Portset supplies products and software for people with visual impairment including DAISY readers, stand-alone document readers and scan-and-read software.

- Website: www.portset.co.uk
- Telephone: +44 (0) 1489 893919
- Email: admin@portset.co.uk

Professional Vision Services supplies a range of access technology including braille displays, braille embossers, screen magnification software, screen reader software and video magnifiers.

- Website: www.professional-vision-services.co.uk
- Telephone: +44 (0) 1462 420751
- Email: sales@professional-vision-services.co.uk

Royal National Institute for the Blind (RNIB) is the largest national charity in the UK working on behalf of people with visual impairment. The RNIB catalogue and on-line shop offers a range of equipment and publications, many of which are suggested in this book. However, RNIB updates its range of equipment and publications regularly, so it is always worth browsing the website for new products and ideas.

Products include: braille and directional compasses, braille embossers, braille notetakers, braille paper, drawing film, thermoform plastic, braille and large print labellers with Dymo tape, scented marker pens, Bumpons, DAISY players, light probes, liquid level indicators, Perkins braillers, Tacti Mark, tactile geometry sets, tactile angle measurers, tactile rulers, thick-line and raised-line writing papers and Wikki Stix.

- Website: www.rnib.org.uk/shop
- Telephone: RNIB Customer Services +44 (0) 845 702 3153
- Email: cservices@rnib.org.uk

Sight and Sound Technology supplies a range of access technology for people with visual impairment, including braille displays, braille embossers, scanning software, screen magnifiers, screen readers and video magnifiers.

- Website: www.sightandsound.co.uk
- Telephone: 0845 634 7979 within the UK or +44 1604 798070 outside the UK
- Email: sales@sightandsound.co.uk

Table 18.1 Tactile signs suppliers

Supplier	Website	Email	Telephone
All Formats	www.allformats.org.uk	signs@qac.ac.uk	+44 (0) 121 428 5050
Architectural Symbols & Signs Ltd	www.as-s.co.uk	quality@as-s.co.uk	+44 (0) 1922 454656
Double Image	www.doubleimage.co.uk	office@doubleimage.co.uk	+44 (0) 141 954 2307
Signs Now	www.signsnow.co.uk	info@signsnow.co.uk	+44 (0) 1902 791201
The Tactile Group	www.tactilesignseurope.com	n/a	+44 (0) 1394 420741

Techno-Vision Systems Ltd supplies a range of equipment for people with visual impairment, including accessible music software, the Book Courier portable audio player, braille embossers, braille paper, braille translation software, large print keyboards, screen readers, screen magnifiers, stand-alone reading machines, a talking dictionary and video magnifiers.

- Website: www.techno-vision.co.uk
- Telephone: +44 (0) 1604 792777
- Email: info@techno-vision.co.uk

Zychem Limited supplies Zy-Fuse heaters and heat swell paper, the T3 Touch Tablet (an audio tactile diagram device) and Smelly vision (a range of scented coloured papers).

- Website: www.zychem.co.uk
- Telephone: +44 (0) 1606 738739
- Email: info@zychem-ltd.co.uk

Educational suppliers

Auto Press Education produces a range of mini whiteboards, including lined whiteboards, an A4 10 × 10 grid whiteboard and an A4 music whiteboard with two large print staves on one side.

- Website: www.autopresseducation.co.uk
- Telephone: 0870 240 3565 within the UK or +44 1604 402299 outside the UK
- Email: info@autopresseducation.co.uk

Bag Books supplies a range of multi-sensory story packs and fiction packs.

- Website: www.bagbooks.org
- Telephone: +44 (0) 20 7385 4021
- Email: office@bagbooks.org

Brunel Microscopes Ltd stocks a wide range of microscopes, including video microscopes.

- Website: www.brunelmicroscopes.co.uk
- Telephone: +44 (0) 1249 462655
- Email: mail@brunelmicroscopes.co.uk

Dancing Dots specialises in accessible music technology for blind users and braille music.

- Website: www.dancingdots.com
- Telephone: USA number (+001) 610 783 6692
- Email: info@dancingdots.com

Davies Sports supplies a range of accessible sports equipment, including goalballs and movement body bags.

- Website: www.daviessports.co.uk
- Telephone: +44 (0) 845 1204 515
- Email: customerservice@daviessports.co.uk

Expressive Software Projects produces accessible educational music software.

- Website: www.espmusic.co.uk
- Telephone: +44 (0) 115 9444140
- Email: sales@espmusic.co.uk

Leap Frog supplies a wide range of education resources suitable for all pupils, including a talking globe.

- Website: www.leapfrogshop.co.uk
- Telephone: 0870 300 0099 within the UK or +44 1254 51567 outside the UK
- Email: help@leapfrogshop.co.uk

Learning Resources supplies a wide range of education resources suitable for all pupils, including cross-section Earth models.

- Website: www.learningresources.co.uk
- Telephone: +44 (0) 1553 762276
- Email: customerservice@learning-resources.co.uk

Philip Harris Education supplies scientific equipment, including video microscopes.

- Website: www.philipharris.co.uk
- Telephone: +44 (0) 845 120 4520
- Email: sales@philipharris.co.uk

Rhino Rugby supplies rugby equipment, including padding for sports posts.

- Website: www.rhinorugby.com
- Telephone: +44 (0) 1822 610500
- Email: sales@rhinorugby.com

TFH Special Needs Toys supplies a range of multi-sensory toys and texture panels.

- Website: www.specialneedstoys.com
- Telephone: +44 (0)1299 827820

The Sensory Company supplies a range of multi-sensory products including equipment for sensory rooms and sensory gardens and Tactile Colour packs (different coloured paper with individual textures designed for each colour).

- Website: www.thesensorycompany.co.uk
- Telephone: +44 (0) 845 838 2233
- Email: webinfo@thesensorycompany.co.uk

UKGE Limited specialises in geological equipment, and has a braille compass available.

- Website: www.ukge.co.uk
- Telephone: 0800 0336 002 within the UK or +44 870 9220091 outside the UK
- Email: sales@ukge.co.uk

Widgit Software produces educational software with emphasis on clear presentation.

- Website: www.widgit.com
- Telephone: +44 (0) 1223 425558
- Email: info@widgit.com

18.2 CD Resources

 Examples of modified learning resource materials and templates for graph paper, writing paper, angle measurers, map outlines, etc. are included on the accompanying CD in MS Word and PDF formats.

Templates

- Angle measurers – large print 180° and 360° angle measurer templates for reproducing on acetate sheets.
- Large print clock face.
- Graph paper – square grids in a range of sizes and colours. Can be used for large print users, or produced on heat swell paper, drawing film or thermoform plastic for tactile users.
- Large print music staves in a range of colours.
- Large print number line in a range of colours.
- Large print number square in a range of colours.
- Paper with dots in a range of colours and sizes.
- Pie chart grids for creating large print or tactile pie charts.
- Ruled paper in a range of colours and sizes.
- Large print periodic table.
- Large print weighing scale face.
- Map outlines – bold outlines of Britain, Ireland, Europe and the continents in a range of colours.

18.3 Obtaining accessible learning resource materials

- Revealweb (www.revealweb.org.uk) is a database of resources in modified formats, as well as an increasing number of electronic and digital versions.
- The RNIB National Library (www.rnib.org.uk) offers a free postal lending service of over 32 000 braille, Moon and giant print titles plus 14 000 braille music scores. The website also offers a range of electronic books and reference materials as well as gateways to information on visual impairment and links to other accessible websites.

Braille

- Braille versions of children's books are available from ClearVision (www.clearvisionproject.org). ClearVision books all have braille, print and pictures making them suitable for sharing. ClearVision also has tactile books available to loan.
- National Blind Children's Society (www.nbcs.org.uk) produces braille books on request at the cost of the original.
- The RNIB National Centre for Tactile Diagrams (www.nctd.org.uk) has a large catalogue of tactile diagrams available to purchase and also offers training courses. Their website has information on designing and producing tactile diagrams.

Large print

- The National Blind Children's Society's (www.nbcs.org.uk) CustomEye books is a large print book service, tailor-made to suit each child's eye condition by providing the correct size of print on the most effective colour of paper.

- Ulverscroft publishers supply large print books (www.ulverscroft.co.uk).

Moon

- For more information about Moon, including a Moon font and how to obtain resources, visit the Moon Literary website (www.moonliteracy.org.uk).

- Children's books in Moon are available to loan from ClearVision (www.clearvisionproject.org).

Audio

- Audio books in DAISY format are available to loan from RNIB's Talking Books Library Service (www.rnib.org.uk/talkingbooks).

- Audio books in CD and cassette format are available to loan from Listening Books (www.listening-books.org.uk) and from Calibre (www.calibre.org.uk).

- Audio books can be purchased from a number of places, including the Talking Book Shop (www.talkingbooks.co.uk).

- Audio newspapers and magazines are available in a choice of formats, including cassette, CD and email, from the Talking Newspaper Association of the UK (www.tnauk.org.uk). For information on local talking newspapers, visit the Talking News Federation website (www.tnf.org.uk).

- For information on DAISY books and DAISY players, visit www.daisy.org.

Art

- i-Map (www.tate.org.uk/imap) is an award-winning arts resource from Tate Online that is aimed at people with visual impairment with a general interest in art as well as teachers and pupils with visual impairment.

- The Living Paintings Trust (www.livingpaintings.org) provides a free library service for people with visual impairment of all ages, enabling access to albums of art collections. Each album contains raised images, audio descriptions and colour reproductions of at least 10 works of art. The collections are designed to group together topics in an interesting and exciting way.

More help

The BECTA VI Forum (http://lists.becta.org.uk/mailman/listinfo/vi-forum) is a useful source of advice on issues relating to teaching pupils with visual impairment in general, and provides a forum for sharing accessible copies of learning resource materials.

Examination and test papers

- The NAA website (www.naa.org.uk/tests) has information about national curriculum tests in England. Past versions of modified **statutory** tests are available from the Modified Test Agency (Statutory) (tel: 0870 321 6727 or email: helpline@pia.co.uk). Past versions of modified **optional** tests are available from the Modified Test Agency (Optional) (tel: 01733 375356 or email: qca@rnib.org.uk).

- Information about access arrangements for general qualifications is available on the Joint Council for Qualifications (JCQ) website (www.jcq.org.uk), and is updated every September.

- *GSE, VCE, GCSE, and GNVQ examinations – specification for the preparation and production of examination papers for candidates with a visual impairment* provides detailed guidance about how exam papers are modified and produced in braille and modified large print, including information on fonts, enlarged simplified and tactile diagrams, and some subject-specific information too. This document is available on RNIB's website (www.rnib.org.uk/curriculum).

- To obtain past copies of modified examinations and other test papers, including published tests, it might be worth placing a request on the online BECTA VI forum to see if another school or support service has a spare copy (http://lists.becta.org.uk/mailman/listinfo/vi-forum).

18.4 Useful organisations and websites

Ability Net (www.abilitynet.org.uk)

Ability Net is a charity offering free advice and information on any aspect of technological aids, especially IT.

Accessible Gaming Rendering Independence (www.agrip.org.uk)

Accessible Gaming Rendering Independence is an organisation working at making mainstream computer games and gaming accessible to people with visual impairment.

Action for Blind People (www.afbp.org)

Action for Blind People is a campaigning organisation offering a range of services for people with visual impairment and out-of-school sports clubs for children with visual impairment.

A-sites (www.nlb-online.info)

A-sites is a National Library for the Blind project offering links to a wide range of accessible websites.

Association of National Specialist Colleges (www.natspec.org.uk)

The Association of National Specialist Colleges' website has a 'college finder' function with contact details for specialist colleges for students with a range of special needs.

Braille Authority of the United Kingdom (www.bauk.org.uk)

BAUK is the braille standards setting body for the United Kingdom. Braille codes are available to download from the website.

British Computer Association for the Blind (www.bcab.org.uk)

BCAB is an organisation of people with visual impairment who use Information and Communications Technology (ICT). Members range from experienced computer professionals to people who are beginning to explore the use of ICT for leisure, study or employment. BCAB provides specialist training, publishes a newsletter and members' CD and supports an active email list which serves as a powerful vehicle for information sharing and networking.

British Retinitis Pigmentosa Society (www.brps.org.uk)

The British Retinitis Pigmentosa Society is a self-help group offering a wide range of services and information, as well as stimulating research.

British Wireless Fund for the Blind (www.blind.org.uk)

The British Wireless Fund for the Blind is a charity supplying adapted radio sets to people with visual impairment.

Guide Dogs for the Blind Association (www.guidedogs.co.uk)

The Guide Dogs for the Blind Association provides guide dogs, mobility and other rehabilitation services for people with visual impairment. Contact your local branch to arrange awareness training.

Henshaws Society for Blind People (www.blind.org.uk)

Henshaws offers a wide range of services including holidays, activities, youth groups and family support services for people with visual impairment across the North of England.

Look (www.look-uk.org)

Look, the National Federation of Families with Visually Impaired Children, is a charity self-help group of parents and families with children with visual impairment.

National Association for Local Societies for Visually Impaired People (www.nalsvi.cswebsites.org)

The National Association for Local Societies for Visually Impaired People is a charity giving information regarding local support organisations for people with visual impairment.

National Blind Children's Society (www.nbcs.org.uk)

NBCS is a charity offering a range of services including education advocacy, large print book service, advice on aids and access technology, activities, holidays and grants.

Nystagmus Network (www.nystagmusnet.org)

The Nystagmus Network is a charity raising awareness, providing information and support to those with nystagmus and promoting research into the condition.

Remap (www.remap.org.uk)

Remap is a charity providing technical aids, free of charge, to people with a range of disabilities.

Royal Blind Society of the United Kingdom (www.royalblindsociety.org)

The Royal Blind Society of the United Kingdom is a charity offering grants, holidays and other support to people with visual impairment on low incomes.

Royal London Society for the Blind (www.rlsb.org.uk)

The Royal London Society for the Blind is a charity offering a family service, with advice, counselling and contact with other families.

Royal National Institute for the Blind (RNIB) (www.rnib.org.uk)

RNIB is the largest national charity in the UK working on behalf of people with visual impairment. The RNIB website provides information on a wide range of issues affecting visual impairment, including information on eye conditions, education, employment, design guidelines, housing, leisure, mobility, music and technology. The online shop has a range of products and publications.

RNIB publishes journals and magazines, including *Insight*, a magazine for all involved in the education of children and young people with visual impairment. *Insight* includes supplements including *Curriculum Bitesize* – a termly eight-page photocopiable resource full of practical tips on making lessons accessible for all pupils with visual impairment.

The RNIB Curriculum Group network exists to assist all those involved in teaching, supporting or advising on the curriculum needs of children and young people with visual impairment. Group meetings for different subject areas are held once or twice each year and are advertised in *Curriculum Bitesize*. For more information, email: curriculum@rnib.org.uk

Scottish Sensory Centre (www.ssc.education.ed.ac.uk)

The Scottish Sensory Centre promotes and supports new development and effective practices in the education of children with visual impairment. Its library has an extensive range of books, videos and journals concerned with the education of children with sensory impairment. Visit the website for information on curriculum access.

Sense (www.sense.org.uk)

Sense is a charity offering support to deafblind people and families with deafblind children.

Sort It (www.sortit.org.uk)

Sort It is a website for 11–16 year olds with a sight problem containing information on leisure activities, advice on school work, equipment, etc. and a message board.

Tiresias (www.tiresias.org)

The Tiresias website provides in-depth information on assistive devices for people with visual impairment, current and future research, technical information, disability organisations and agencies, sources of research, funding, publications, standards and legislation.

Torch Trust for the Blind (www.torchtrust.org)

Torch Trust is a Christian organisation for people with visual impairment. The Torch Trust produces Christian literature in accessible formats and promotes Christian fellowship with and among people with visual impairment.

Victa (www.victa.org.uk)

Victa is a charity offering funding to individuals, organisations and other bodies (including schools) for equipment and services for young people with visual impairment.

Vision 2020 (www.vision2020uk.org.uk)

Vision 2020 is a charity acting as an umbrella organisation promoting collaboration and cooperation between organisations working in the field of visual impairment.

Visugate (www.visugate.org)

Visugate is a free online gateway to electronic information about visual impairment.

Glossary

Access technology – Access technology encompasses a range of equipment that enables people with visual impairment to interact with technology. The terms 'adaptive technology', 'assistive technology' and 'enabling technology' also refer to methods for people with visual impairment to access computers. Access technology includes braille notetakers, braille displays, screen reader software, screen magnifier software, stand-alone document readers and video magnifiers (CCTVs).

Accessibility – Many definitions exist of accessibility, most of which emphasise ease of use. Generally, increasing accessibility involves reducing barriers to use, e.g. providing braille, audio or large print versions of learning resource materials and displays, etc.; applying accessibility settings on computer displays; enabling hardware and software to be used with screen readers; removing physical barriers in classrooms, etc.

Accessible print – A design approach to making printed material accessible to as wide a range of people as possible. Also known as 'clear print'.

Amanuensis – Pupils with visual impairment sometimes dictate their work to an amanuensis, particularly in examination situations. Also known as a 'scribe'.

Binca – Open-weave fabric often used for teaching sewing to beginners.

Brailon – See Thermoform plastic.

Braille – A tactile reading system based on a grid of six dots. Braille is used by people with severe visual impairment who are unable to access print.

Braille display – Braille displays are lightweight electro-mechanical devices that protrude from underneath the front of a standard computer keyboard. The device presents the information on screen as braille, a line at a time.

Braille embosser – A computer-driven braille printer that presses braille dots into paper and other thin materials.

Braille notetaker – A portable device that uses a six-key entry system to take notes, record and organise information and produces output in either braille or print, as required.

Braille paper – Heavyweight paper used in Perkins braillers and embossers. Available in library/Perkins size (11″×11″) or A4 size.

Bumpons – Simple raised bumps supplied on self-adhesive sheets in a range of sizes and colours for marking different equipment.

CCTVs – See Video magnifiers.

Contractions – Grade 2 braille uses abbreviations or short forms of many words and letter combinations.

DAISY – Digital Accessible Information System. A DAISY book is a digital audio book that allows the user to navigate as a print user would navigate a print book. DAISY books can be read using a DAISY Talking Book player or DAISY software on a computer.

Drawing film – Thin plastic film that can be used for tactile 'drawing' with a stylus or ballpoint pen. Drawing film can also be used to create thermoformed diagrams in a thermoform machine. Also known as 'German film' and 'plastic film'.

Dymo guns – Specialist dymo guns can be used to produce braille and large print labels.

Dymo tape – Dymo tape is used with a large print or braille Dymo gun, all available from RNIB (www.rnib.org.uk).

Flexi Curves – Used to produce tactile curves. Made of a PVC outer casing with a core of lead, available from art suppliers.

Functional vision – The use we make of our vision in everyday life. All children with visual impairment have their functional vision assessed by a specialist teacher for visual impairment.

German film – See Drawing film.

Grade 1 braille – The simplest form of braille, where each braille cell represents a single print letter.

Grade 2 braille – Grade 2 braille uses contractions of many words and letter combinations.

Heat swell – Heat swell diagrams are originated by printing or photocopying an image onto specially coated paper and feeding it through a heat machine that raises all black ink.

JAWS – Screen reader software.

Large print – A printed document with a minimum font size of 14 point.

Learning environment – Throughout this book, the term 'learning environment' is used to denote the physical and social environment for all learning activity.

Low vision aid – A low vision aid is any piece of equipment used by people with visual impairment to enhance their vision. Often used to refer to optical magnifiers, telescopes, video magnifiers, task lighting, liquid level indicators, Bumpons, etc.

Minolta – Heat swell paper.

Modify – Throughout this book, the term 'modify' is used to denote making printed and electronic information accessible for pupils with visual impairment.

Modified print – Printed materials with visual layout modified for pupils with visual impairment, e.g. illustrations and diagrams omitted, simplified or replaced with written description or models.

Moon – An alternative reading method to braille, primarily used by people with visual impairment and additional difficulties, such as learning difficulties or poor finger sensitivity.

Newclay – Reinforced air-drying modelling clay that can be painted and treated with varnish to give a long-lasting final product.

OCR – Optical character recognition software that turns printed text into digital text, which can be magnified or read by a screen reader.

Perkins brailler – A mechanical machine with nine keys similar to a simple typewriter for producing braille manually.

Photocopy enlargement – Enlarging materials on a photocopier without modifying the visual layout.

Plastic film – see Drawing film.

QTVI – Qualified teacher for visual impairment. See Specialist teacher for visual impairment.

Residual vision – The useful sight a person with visual impairment has. Most people with visual impairment have some residual vision.

Screen reader software – Screen reader software speaks text aloud, in a synthesised voice, through computer speakers.

Screen magnifier software – Screen magnifier software zooms in on the computer screen detail, making it big enough to see, so that users can read text without straining their eyes or adopting a poor seating posture. Colours, contrast and brightness can be altered to suit individual needs.

Sensory support service – Local authorities in the UK have sensory support services, which employ specialist teachers for visual impairment.

Shortcut keys – Keyboard shortcuts enable users to operate computer functions quickly using the keyboard instead of a mouse.

Specialist teacher for visual impairment – Specialist teachers for visual impairment have completed a qualification for working with children and young people with visual impairment.

Spur wheel – A small embossing tool for creating tactile lines.

Supernova – Software that combines screen reading and screen magnification.

Tactile – Something that is accessed through touch, rather than other senses, e.g. a tactile diagram is a raised diagram that may have a variety of textures.

Tacti Mark – A liquid plastic that when dabbed on, dries to produce raised permanent shapes, which are highly visible.

Task lighting – Lighting positioned to fall directly onto an area of work, perhaps from a spot or desk lamp.

Thermoformed diagrams – Thermoformed diagrams are produced from a tactile original made as a collage, using materials such as wire, string and sandpaper. The collage is copied onto plastic sheets (see Thermoform plastic) in a vacuum-forming thermoform machine.

Thermoform plastic – Plastic sheets on which thermoformed diagrams are reproduced. Also known as 'Brailon' and 'plastic film'.

Tiger embosser – Tiger embossers produce simple diagrams using raised dots on standard braille paper, and enable text and diagrams to be embossed on the same page.

VIPs – A common abbreviation for very important person, which is also used as an abbreviation for visually impaired person.

Visiting teacher – See Specialist teacher for visual impairment.

Visual impairment – Throughout this book, the term 'visual impairment' is used to include pupils with a range of visual impairments, including pupils who are registered blind or partially sighted.

Wikki Stix – Wax-covered string that sticks to itself and to smooth surfaces. Useful for marking tactile lines, graph curves, etc.

Bibliography

Arter, C., Mason, H. L., McCall, S., McLinden, M. and Stone, J. M. (1999) *Children with Visual Impairment in Mainstream Settings*. London: David Fulton Publishers.

Ashman, H. and Menken, A. (1982) *Little Shop of Horrors* (musical).

Booth, T. and Ainscow, M. (2002) *Index for Inclusion: Developing Learning and Participation in Schools*. Bristol: Centre for Studies on Inclusive Education.

Brown, N. (2001) 'Microscopy for the Visually Impaired', www.rnibncw.ac.uk/?_id=290, (viewed 21.07.06).

Brown, N. (2004) 'Teaching light to students with a visual impairment', RNIB *Curriculum Close-Up* (19): 10–12.

Carle, E. (1970) *The Very Hungry Caterpillar*. London: Puffin Books.

Centre for Studies on Inclusive Education. 'Ten reasons for inclusion,' http://inclusion.uwe.ac.uk/csie/10rsns.htm, (viewed 21.07.06).

Copyright (Visually Impaired Persons) Act 2002, c. 33. London: HMSO.

Gardiner, A. and Perkins, C. (2003) 'Here is the beech tree: understanding tactile maps in the field', *The Cartographic Journal* 40(3): 277–282.

Hinton, R. (1988) *Thermoformed Tactile Diagrams – A Manual for Teachers and Technicians*. London: RNIB.

Joint Council for Qualifications (2005) *GCE, VCE, GCSE and GNVQ examinations specification for the preparation and production of examination papers for candidates with a visual impairment*. London: Joint Council for Qualifications.

Mason, H. (2001) *Spotlight on SEN: Visual Impairment*. London: NASEN.

Mason, H., McCall, S., Arter, C., McLinden, M. and Stone, J. (1997) *Visual Impairment: Access to Education for Children and Young People*. London: David Fulton Publishers.

McGough, R. (1985) *Sky in the Pie*. London: Puffin.

Naish, L., Clunies-Ross, L. and Bell, J. (2004) *Exploring Access in Mainstream: How to Audit your School Environment, Focusing on the Needs of Pupils who have Visual Impairment*. London: RNIB.

RNIB (2001) *Painting from a New Perspective: Six Artists and their Experiences of Sight Loss*. London: RNIB.

RNIB (2001) *Well Prepared*. London: RNIB.

RNIB (2004) *Written Off*. London: RNIB.

RNIB (2006) *See It Right*. London: RNIB.

RNIB 'Accessible Information: Copyright (Visually Impaired Persons) Act 2002', www.rnib.org.uk/xpedio/groups/public/documents/publicwebsite/public_cvipsact2002.hcsp, (viewed 21.07.06).

RNIB and Vocaleyes (2003) *Museums, Galleries and Heritage Sites: Improving Access for Blind and Partially Sighted People. The Talking Images Guide*. London: RNIB.

Russell, W. (1977) *Our Day Out*. London: BBC.

Warren, D. H. (1994) *Blindness in Children: An Individual Differences Approach*. New York: Cambridge University Press.

Wesseling, L. (2004) *Focus on Braille Music*. London: Musicians in Focus.

Index